Just a Few Miles South

TIMELESS RECIPES FROM OUR FAVORITE PLACES

Just a Few Miles South

OUITA MICHEL
SARA GIBBS *and* GENIE GRAF

Illustrated by
BRENNA FLANNERY

Foreword by
SILAS HOUSE

FIRESIDE INDUSTRIES

Published by Fireside Industries
An imprint of the University Press of Kentucky

Editorial and Sales Offices:
The University Press of Kentucky
663 South Limestone Street,
Lexington, Kentucky 40508-4008
www.kentuckypress.com

Cover and interior design by Jennifer L. Witzke

Library of Congress Cataloging-in-Publication Data
Names: Michel, Ouita, author. | Gibbs, Sara T., author. |
Graf, Genie, author. | Flannery, Brenna, illustrator.
Title: Just a few miles South: timeless recipes from our favorite places /
Ouita Michel, Sara Gibbs, and Genie Graf; illustrated by Brenna Flannery;
foreword by Silas House.
Description: Lexington, Kentucky: Fireside Industries, [2021]
Identifiers: LCCN 2020053352 | ISBN 9781950564095 (hardcover) | ISBN
9781950564101 (pdf) | ISBN 9781950564118 (epub)
Subjects: LCSH: Cooking, American—Southern style. | Cooking—Southern States. |
LCGFT: Cookbooks.
Classification: LCC TX715.2.S68 M5 2021 | DDC 641.5975—dc23

CONTENTS

2 Building Blocks for Sandwiches

3 Wallace Station's Famous Sandwiches

4 Windy Corner's Famous Po-Boys

5 Burgers

6 Soups, Stews, and Salads

7 Brownies, Bars, and Cookies

8 Pie Supper

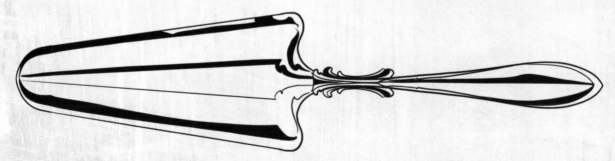

✑ FOREWORD

"Food is love," Ouita Michel says all the time. She signs letters this way. She says this in speeches and conversations. And that love is present in every recipe in this book, whether she is talking about the ache of missing her mother's sandwiches or the profound attachment she feels to Kentucky. "I love the sight of the moon rising and the sound of the horses snorting as their grooms lather them up and comb their manes, getting them ready for the coming day," she writes, capturing a morning in bluegrass country as she makes biscuit sandwiches and stirs up a batch of grits for the workers. On every page it is clear: Ouita loves to feed people.

Ouita is much more than a chef and a restaurant owner. She is a community builder and an activist for the transformative power of food, and perhaps best of all, she is one of those people whose mere presence makes the world a better place. I write that without hyperbole, because I know it to be true from experience. When you are with Ouita, you can't help but feel the compassion in everything she does. You also can't help but learn: about the history of food, about the way a chef thinks about taste, about fairness and equity in the food industry. She is a natural teacher at heart. And she is someone who is not afraid to talk about love in this cynical time, when so many others claim that love is too precious a thought to articulate. Yet she is never precious. Instead, she is firm in her beliefs, even while she is modest, unassuming, and deeply empathetic.

That's why this book is so important: *Just a Few Miles South* makes readers feel like they're in the kitchen with Ouita. This cookbook is not just fun to read and full of beautiful illustrations; it actually makes you want to cook. It is not daunting or pretentious; in fact, it is completely down-home, just like Ouita is: straightforward but kindhearted. It took me a while to read *Just a Few Miles South* because I kept stopping to savor the words and savor the prospect of the dishes I'd be able to make. The first recipe I tried is the one for tuna salad, which contains ingredients easily found in just about anyone's pantry and is absolutely delicious. It's so delicious, in fact, that there must be something special going on. I think it might be that some of the love Ouita exudes comes through in every carefully chosen ingredient. I think her desire to better the world by feeding it has eased its way into every recipe.

Reading *Just a Few Miles South* also makes us more conscientious without preaching to us. "I consider the local farmer my partner in expressing the taste and cuisine of Kentucky," Ouita tells us at one point. "This commitment to locally raised beef helps farmers increase their efficiency and reduce food waste, encouraging consumption of the entire animal." Ouita knows that being a good neighbor is one of the most important things we can be, and her example fosters goodwill among those who know her, those who visit her restaurants, and now, those who read her book.

Just a Few Miles South is a tour of Kentucky and a praise song for place. It's a meditation on the importance of food in our lives and the importance of being a good neighbor in ways big and small. Of course it's a guide to cooking some great dishes, but it's also an introduction to Ouita Michel's fine collection of restaurants, which everyone should visit. Here in Kentucky, we all count Ouita as one of the treasures of our commonwealth, and now this book will allow many others to meet her and learn about the fine work she is doing for our place and our palates.

Silas House

INTRODUCTION

About ten years ago, after twenty years of cooking and several years of owning restaurants, I realized that I wanted my work to reflect this Kentucky place that I love so much. I wanted to express my love for Kentucky with ingredients that are locally produced by our farming community. I wanted to express it through location and setting—siting my restaurants along scenic byways where Thoroughbreds frolic in vibrantly green paddocks and housing them in old buildings, some plain and simple and others crafted of grand limestone in the heart of downtown. I wanted to express it with recipes that are time honored—some so old that they are new to young folks, and some that Kentuckians are lucky enough to eat nearly every day.

Among my small group of family-owned restaurants, the greatest innovation might be that we refuse to bow to the omnipresent convenience fare that most restaurants have come to rely on in our fast-food culture. We bake sandwich bread ourselves, using flour from an eighth-generation mill located just minutes away. Our staple dish, a best seller across the board, is an iconic Kentucky favorite: soup beans and cornbread. We make skillet cornbread and hoecakes in well-worn cast-iron pans and on the griddle. We grind up pimiento cheese and bake sorghum cookies and biscuits. A local pig farmer provides the pork for our spicy breakfast sausage, bacon, and country ham. We roll wild-caught catfish in Kentucky cornmeal and fry it up. Our hamburgers are made from locally raised beef.

This book captures the best recipes from my sandwich shops Wallace Station, near Midway, and Windy Corner Market, off the scenic Paris Pike in northern Fayette County, and from the Midway Bakery and Café. Many of these recipes are also served at Smithtown Seafood, a hole-in-the-wall fried fish shop, and Zim's Café, a Kentucky diner. Some of the recipes began in the kitchen of Holly Hill Inn, my first restaurant, which we fondly call the mother ship. They have been made thousands and thousands of times by countless cooks. For this book, Sara Gibbs scaled down, tested, and retested each recipe, making sure it would work for a home kitchen. Then we sent the recipes to a group of folks and asked them to make the dishes in their own kitchens. Feedback ensued, and the process was repeated until we had crafted a book of recipes that are rock solid, well tested, and, most importantly, readily consumed. We hope it becomes one of the most trusted and most frequently used books in your kitchen. Brenna Flannery provided the beautiful illustrations, inspired by these recipes and from whence they came.

My husband, Chris, and I built the kind of restaurants we would hope to find on our own journeys and adventures: a little quirky, off the beaten path, an authentic expression of place, and full of deliciousness. We are grateful for all the hands that joined with ours on this journey, for those that raise a fork at our tables, and for those that prepare and serve our food every day. Food can indeed be love when it is made with so much care.

1

Breakfast

Stone ground grits from down the road, shaved Kentucky country ham,
Salty-spicy breakfast sausage sold in a bag, not a puck,
Bright yellow egg yolks from a brown shell,
Buttermilk biscuit with a drop of sorghum or local honey,
These are the quintessential ingredients for an
old-fashioned Kentucky breakfast.

— *Ouita Michel*

My restaurants Wallace Station and Windy Corner Market are situated in some of the most beautiful farmland in the world. In the early morning, the mist rises above the gently rolling, brilliantly green pastures running with foals—the sight is breathtaking. During the horse sales at Fasig-Tipton in Lexington, we are on the grounds by 5:00 a.m., making breakfast for the early-morning rush. Stable hands, trainers, and owners come in for steaming cups of coffee and piled-high biscuit sandwiches or plates of grits and eggs. I love the sight of the moon rising and the sound of the horses snorting as their grooms lather them up and comb their manes, getting them ready for the coming day.

THE BREAKFAST PLATE AT WINDY CORNER MARKET

A breakfast plate is an anytime-in-the-morning pleasure, hearty and filling, savored with a cup of coffee and shared with family or friends. I serve this big meal, made with locally sourced ingredients, at my country store–style café in the storied Thoroughbred countryside just off Paris Pike in northern Fayette County. Come hungry to the table for a plate of local eggs, country ham or Stone Cross Farm bacon or sausage, cheese grits, home fries, biscuits, and pancakes. And don't forget a side of sausage gravy.

Weisenberger Mill Cheese Grits

Grits are traditional fare in Kentucky, and they are served every day at Windy Corner Market and every weekend at Holly Hill Inn. At all my restaurants, we use only Weisenberger Mill stone-ground grits, produced just down the road from Midway.

Leftover grits can be poured into sheet pans and cooled, then sliced, dusted in flour or cornmeal, and pan-fried for crispy grits cakes, which make a nice side dish or can be served with poached eggs. Cut them into smaller squares for crispy grits croutons, which are a great accompaniment for a Southern Caesar salad.

At Holly Hill Inn, large pots of grits are allowed to sit for long periods of time, usually 1½ hours, using only the warmth from the pilot light. Sous chef emeritus Lisa Laufer describes this method as "letting them swell." Most home cooks will want to cook grits over a very low heat to save time.

We prefer to grate our own cheese. Preshredded cheese is mixed with cornstarch to prevent clumping and has a muddled flavor.

1 cup Weisenberger Mill stone-ground grits

2 cups water

1½ cups whole milk

½ cup heavy cream

1½ teaspoons kosher salt

¼ teaspoon cayenne

1½ cups (about 6 ounces) shredded sharp white or yellow Cheddar cheese

Bring water, milk, and cream to a hard boil in a 4-quart stockpot with a tight-fitting lid. Add grits, reduce heat, and stir until they come back to a simmer. Cover the grits and reduce the heat as low as possible. Cook 30–40 minutes, stirring occasionally to make sure the grits don't scorch on the bottom. When thickened, stir in salt and cayenne, then stir in shredded cheese and blend thoroughly. Remove from heat, cover, and rest a few minutes until the cheese has melted completely. Taste for seasoning. Serve warm.

Makes about 4½ cups or 8 generous servings.

Cheese grits can also be made in a slow cooker. Add grits, water, milk, cream, and salt to the cooker, and set on high. Stir every 30 minutes or so for 2 hours—yes, you must break the "Never lift the lid!" rule. Then set on low and cook another 2 hours until the grits are tender. It might seem like the grits will never thicken, but then, all of a sudden, they tighten up. Stir in cayenne and cheese and serve.

Steve-O's Red-Eye Gravy

Steve Rose, a longtime sous chef at Windy Corner Market, learned to cook at the hip of his grandmother, Grace Rose. She was from Stanton, Kentucky, and cooked at a popular restaurant called Dalton's. He remembers going to work with her when he was quite small and drinking the cream from the glass pitcher while she sipped her black coffee. Steve-O starts his red-eye gravy with bacon fat, "enough to get it started frying, but not really enough to change the flavor." When asked about adding sweeteners, he said, "Honey, sorghum is for biscuits, not for gravy." However, other cooks think this strong, salty gravy needs a little something to smooth out the flavor, so the choice is yours.

1 tablespoon bacon fat

¼ cup (1 ounce) country ham scraps

1 cup brewed coffee

Pinch smoked paprika

Kosher salt and freshly ground black pepper to taste

Sorghum to taste (optional)

Heat bacon fat in a small, heavy skillet over medium-high heat. Add country ham scraps and cook until dark in color and rendered. Add coffee, smoked paprika, and salt and pepper and bring to a simmer, stirring and scraping any browned bits from the bottom of the pan. Cook 5 minutes until dark reddish brown, and season with sorghum if you wish. Strain and serve on pan-browned country ham slices or over cheese grits.

Makes about ¾ cup or 4 servings.

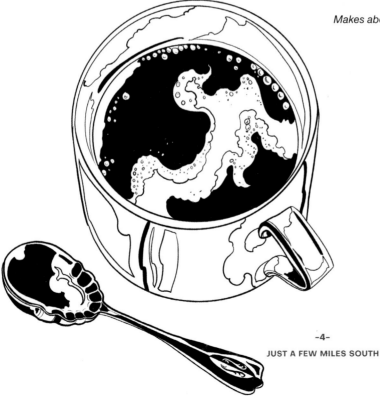

Buttermilk Biscuits

Biscuits are a Kentucky tradition at all meals, not just breakfast. We use cocktail-size biscuits with country ham and apple butter as appetizers, and we serve larger biscuits with sorghum butter for dinner or breakfast. They also make great breakfast sandwiches. Using a cheese grater to grate the butter helps integrate it into the biscuit dough.

2 cups all-purpose flour, sifted

2 teaspoons baking powder

½ teaspoon baking soda

½ teaspoon iodized salt

1 teaspoon sugar

½ cup (1 stick) unsalted butter, frozen

⅔ cup cold buttermilk

Preheat oven to 375 degrees F.

In a large bowl, whisk together flour, baking powder, baking soda, salt, and sugar.

Grate frozen butter directly into the flour mixture. Stir in buttermilk and form a dough.

Turn out onto a floured surface and knead once or twice. Roll out the dough on a floured surface to ½-inch thick and cut into rounds.

Use a 2-inch cutter for cocktail biscuits and a 2½- to 3-inch cutter for larger biscuits.

Bake 11–12 minutes for cocktail biscuits and 13–14 minutes for larger biscuits.

Makes 14 small biscuits or 8 large ones.

Sorghum Butter

This butter is a sweet counterpart to a salty country ham biscuit or a special finish for hoecakes or pancakes. Swirl the same amount of cold butter pieces into hot sorghum to make a caramel sauce.

½ cup (1 stick) unsalted butter, softened

¼ cup sorghum

Blend butter and sorghum in a food processor until well blended and creamy.

Makes a generous ½ cup.

Sausage Gravy

Sausage gravy is popular in both the North and the South. This version gets its extra-special flavor from a spicy sausage made by Stone Cross Farm in nearby Spencer County. A medium-spicy breakfast sausage provides just the right amount of pepper and sage for a flavorful gravy. Use your favorite sausage, and adjust the amount of salt and pepper as needed. A pinch of rubbed sage can punch up the flavor even more.

---

1 pound Stone Cross Farm medium breakfast sausage or other medium-spicy breakfast sausage

½ cup all-purpose flour

1 quart whole milk (or more to taste)

1 teaspoon kosher salt

½ teaspoon freshly ground black pepper

Place a large, heavy skillet over medium heat. Add sausage in small pieces and cook until brown and no longer pink, breaking up the meat with a wooden spoon as it cooks.

Sprinkle flour over the cooked sausage and stir until the meat is coated with flour and beginning to brown, about 1 minute. Pour in milk and mix well. Cook, stirring constantly, until the gravy begins to bubble and thicken. Stir in salt and pepper, reduce heat, and simmer about 10 minutes, stirring often. If the gravy is too thick, add milk.

Taste for seasoning, then pour over warm buttermilk biscuits.

Makes about 5 cups or 8 generous servings.

I like to start my milk in a double boiler, so I don't burn or scorch the gravy. I brown the sausage in a cast-iron skillet and add the browned sausage bits to the hot milk. I like to make my roux with bacon fat. That's how my grandma Grace Rose taught me, using equal parts bacon fat and flour. While the roux is cooking, I scrape up any browned bits from the bottom of the skillet so they will flavor the gravy. I whisk the roux into the hot milk mixture and let it cook until it thickens. You can watch it change in density. As for portions, I am generous with my sausage gravy. My grandma taught me that, too.

—Steve Rose, Windy Corner Market

BREAKFAST SANDWICHES

Wallace Station began making breakfast sandwiches because the locals who worked on nearby horse farms requested them. The restaurant's very first customer was Merv Leckbee, a former jockey and night watchman at Three Chimneys Farm, down the road on Old Frankfort Pike. Merv would finish his shift and show up at Wallace Station's door every morning for breakfast. He dressed up like a leprechaun for the restaurant's first St. Patrick's Day and danced outside to attract visitors. After Merv died, his wife, Roberta, gave us a little knitted leprechaun that sat on a shelf at Wallace Station for years. Wallace Station honored Merv by naming the Ham and Jalapeño Panini after him (see chapter 3).

Ouita's Sardou Panini

Eggs Sardou is a classic Creole dish created in New Orleans. It is named for a famous dramatist, Victorien Sardou, who visited the Big Easy in the early 1900s. This decadent dish is believed to have originated at Antoine's, with poached eggs, hollandaise sauce, artichoke bottoms, truffles, ham, and anchovies.

Years ago, I had a side job as a consultant to a major restaurant chain. One of the recipes I developed for the chain was the Sardou Panini, but the restaurant rejected it. It has become one of Wallace Station's most popular sandwiches—the customers love it. Here is a simplified reimagining of the dish, which makes an inspired vegetarian breakfast sandwich.

8 slices white or whole wheat bread

1 cup Spinach Artichoke Spread (recipe follows)

¾ cup Hollandaise Butter (see later in this chapter)

6 large eggs, beaten

Canola oil for cooking eggs

Butter oil for grilling (equal parts melted butter and canola oil)

For each sandwich, lay out 2 slices of bread. Cover 1 slice with 3–4 tablespoons Spinach Artichoke Spread and the other with 2 tablespoons Hollandaise Butter. Set aside.

Heat an 8-inch nonstick skillet over medium-low heat. Add a small amount of canola oil and swirl to cover the bottom of the pan. Pour in one-quarter of the egg mixture and cook as a small omelet, just until set. Slide out the omelet and place it on the bread slice with the Spinach Artichoke Spread. Cover with the remaining slice of bread. Brush the bread with butter oil and place in a nonstick skillet or griddle over medium-high heat. Brown on both sides and serve warm.

Repeat with remaining ingredients.

Serves 4.

Spinach Artichoke Spread

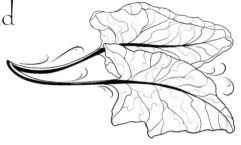

1 tablespoon heavy cream

2 teaspoons unsalted butter, softened

1 (8-ounce) package cream cheese, softened

½ cup mayonnaise

1 teaspoon minced garlic

1 (10-ounce) box frozen chopped spinach, thawed and squeezed dry

1 (14-ounce) can artichoke hearts (in water), drained and chopped

¾ cup shredded Parmesan cheese

¼ teaspoon kosher salt

Pinch cayenne pepper

¼ teaspoon ground sage

¼ teaspoon white pepper

Place cream, butter, cream cheese, mayonnaise, and minced garlic in the bowl of an electric mixer. Mix on medium until well blended. Add remaining ingredients and mix briefly. Artichoke hearts should still be slightly chunky. Taste for seasoning. Use immediately or chill. Leftover Spinach Artichoke Spread can be used as a baked dip, topped with a generous sprinkle of Parmesan cheese.

Makes about 1 quart.

Hollandaise Butter

3 hard-cooked egg yolks

2 tablespoons fresh lemon juice

4 tablespoons unsalted butter, softened

½ teaspoon iodized salt

¼ teaspoon cayenne pepper

1 tablespoon water

¼ cup olive oil

Place egg yolks, lemon juice, butter, salt, cayenne pepper, and water in a blender and mix until smooth, stirring and scraping the sides as necessary. Drizzle in olive oil and blend until smooth and well mixed. Taste for seasoning, and chill until spreadable.

Makes ¾ cup.

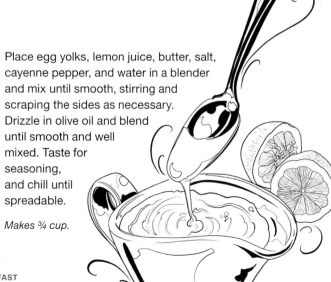

Bluegrass Benedict

The Bluegrass Benedict at Holly Hill Inn is popular, so we came up with a more casual version for Wallace Station. This hearty breakfast sandwich is a handheld eggs Benedict with the addition of Kentucky's favorite breakfast meat: country ham. The lemon-spiked Hollandaise Butter is a versatile spread that can be used to enhance any sandwich or canapé.

8 slices white or whole wheat bread

¾ cup Hollandaise Butter
(recipe previous page)

4 ounces thinly sliced country ham

8 thin tomato slices

6 large eggs, beaten

Canola oil for cooking eggs

Butter oil for grilling (equal parts
melted butter and canola oil)

For each sandwich, lay out 2 slices of bread. Cover 1 slice with 3 tablespoons Hollandaise Butter. Set aside.

Heat a nonstick skillet over medium-low heat. Add a small amount of canola oil and swirl to cover the bottom of the pan. Pour in one-quarter of the egg mixture and cook as a small omelet, just until set. Slide out the omelet and place it on the bread slice with the Hollandaise Butter. Top with 1 ounce country ham and 2 tomato slices. Cover with the remaining slice of bread. Brush the bread with butter oil and place in a nonstick skillet or griddle over medium-high heat. Brown on both sides and serve warm.

Repeat with remaining ingredients.

Serves 4.

Breakfast Sandwich Omelets

We like to make small omelets for breakfast sandwiches because they lie flat on the bread and make building the sandwich easier. Ideally, an omelet should be yellow and barely golden brown in places. A lower heat creates a more tender egg with a moist interior. For our generous breakfast sandwiches, 1½ eggs make the perfect size omelet.

6 large eggs

Kosher salt and freshly ground black pepper

Unsalted butter for cooking eggs (olive oil or bacon drippings work well, too)

Whisk eggs with a fork until well blended. Lightly season with salt and pepper and whisk again. Be sparing with salt because most breakfast sandwiches include salty cured or smoked meat.

Heat an 8-inch nonstick skillet over medium heat for several minutes. Add 1 teaspoon unsalted butter and swirl it in the pan as it melts so the entire surface is coated. Pour in 6 tablespoons of the whisked egg mixture (this equals 1½ large eggs) and let it cook about 30 seconds, until the edges turn opaque. Using a silicone or heat-resistant rubber spatula, pull the edges of the omelet toward the center and tip the pan so that the uncooked egg fills the empty space and begins to cook. Continue doing this until the egg is almost firm throughout. Turn and let the omelet finish cooking undisturbed 10–20 seconds, until no liquid egg remains. You can also finish the omelet off the stove, using the pan's residual heat to cook the last bit of egg. Slide the omelet out onto a sandwich or onto a plate until ready to use.

Repeat with remaining egg mixture to make 4 sandwich omelets.

I always have one 8-inch nonstick pan designated just for eggs in my kitchen. This is the result of working in a busy breakfast restaurant for six years. Those morning egg cooks took care of their pans, even going so far as to lock them in a filing cabinet at the end of their shifts so the evening sauté cooks wouldn't ruin the finish. (In turn, the evening cooks hid their dry, clean towels above the ceiling tiles, but that's another story.) It is vital to have an unscarred finish on your egg pans when you are juggling three or more pans at one time.

If you prefer to use a fried egg on your breakfast sandwich, I suggest breaking the yolk before turning it so it will cook through, avoiding the messiness. —Sara Gibbs

Breakfast Sandwich Baked Omelets

Another technique that works for a crowd is to bake a large omelet in the oven and then cut it into squares. These baked omelet portions work beautifully on biscuits or English muffins, which is how the Midway Bakery serves its breakfast sandwiches. The recipe given here has a rather neutral flavor profile, since the other sandwich ingredients add to the dish, but you can incorporate whatever flavors you like.

9 large eggs

½ cup heavy cream

½ cup shredded Cheddar cheese

½ teaspoon kosher salt

½ teaspoon freshly ground black pepper

Preheat oven to 350 degrees F. Coat a 9-by-9-inch baking dish with nonstick spray. Set aside.

In a medium bowl, beat eggs until well blended. Whisk in cream and Cheddar cheese, and season with salt and pepper. Pour into the baking dish.

Bake until puffed and set, about 20 minutes.

Makes 9 small squares for biscuit sandwiches or 4 large squares for bread sandwiches.

QUICHE

Roasted Sweet Potato, Gruyère, and Caramelized Onion Quiche

Midway Bakery staffer Justin Traugott created this vegetarian quiche. It is a nice change from the typical vegetarian quiche, which usually features spinach, broccoli, or mushrooms. We love to use sweet potatoes in both sweet and savory dishes, especially roasted.

1 Midway Bakery All-Butter Pie Crust (see index)

1 medium sweet potato (about 9 ounces), peeled

1 tablespoon canola oil

Kosher salt and freshly ground black pepper to taste

1 tablespoon unsalted butter

½ sweet onion, thinly sliced

Kosher salt and freshly ground black pepper to taste

1–2 tablespoons white wine for deglazing

1 cup (4 ounces) shredded Gruyère cheese

6 large eggs

1 cup half-and-half

¼ teaspoon iodized salt

¼ teaspoon freshly ground black pepper

Pinch cayenne pepper (optional)

Place the dough in a 9-inch deep-dish pie plate, fold extra pastry over the edges, and flute. Freeze at least 15 minutes.

Preheat oven to 400 degrees F. Cut sweet potato into slices ¼ inch thick. Toss with canola oil and season with salt and pepper. Turn out onto a baking sheet and bake 20 minutes, until fork tender. Set aside to cool.

While the sweet potato is baking, heat a small skillet over medium-high heat. Add butter to melt, then add sliced onion. Season lightly with salt and pepper and sauté, stirring often. Once onions begin to brown, reduce heat and cook until dark golden brown. Deglaze the pan with white wine and stir until wine has evaporated. Remove from heat and set aside to cool.

Reduce oven to 350 degrees F.

Cover the bottom of the frozen pie crust with sweet potatoes, then layer on caramelized onions and Gruyère. Set aside.

In a small bowl, whisk together eggs, half-and-half, salt, pepper, and cayenne, if desired. Pour over ingredients in pie crust.

Place the quiche on a parchment-lined baking sheet and bake 50–55 minutes, until the filling is completely set and does not jiggle. Remove from the oven and rest at room temperature 20 minutes before serving, so the slices will cut cleanly.

Serves 6–8.

Country Ham, Apple, and Cheddar Quiche

The Midway Bakery makes quiche year-round, using whatever ingredients are available. Because we always have country ham and apples on hand, this combination is easy to put together quickly. Freezing the pie crust eliminates the need to blind-bake. Quiche is served all day at the Midway Bakery, Windy Corner Market, and Wallace Station.

1 Midway Bakery All-Butter Pie Crust (see index)

3 green onions, thinly sliced

½ Gala apple, peeled and finely chopped

½ cup shredded Cheddar cheese (about 2 ounces)

1 cup (4 ounces) finely chopped country ham

6 large eggs

1 cup half-and-half

¼ teaspoon iodized salt

¼ teaspoon freshly ground black pepper

Preheat oven to 350 degrees F. Place the dough in a 9-inch deep-dish pie plate, fold extra pastry over the edges, and flute. Freeze at least 15 minutes.

Remove the dough from the freezer and assemble ingredients. Cover the bottom of the pie crust with green onions, then layer on apples, Cheddar, and country ham. Set aside.

In a small bowl, whisk together eggs, half-and-half, salt, and pepper. Pour over ingredients in pie crust.

Place the quiche on a parchment-lined baking sheet and bake 45–55 minutes, until the filling is completely set and does not jiggle. Remove from the oven and rest at room temperature 20 minutes before serving, so the slices will cut cleanly.

Serves 6–8.

Chorizo Breakfast Hash Quiche

Holiday weekends are made for brunch. This spicy, filling quiche was created by Midway Bakery staff for New Year's Day orders. Local chorizo browned with fresh vegetables gives this quiche loads of flavor and a little heat. Thinly sliced green onions and sour cream are the perfect finish. Serve with fresh fruit and buttermilk biscuits.

1 Midway Bakery All-Butter Pie Crust (see index)

4 ounces fresh Mexican chorizo

½ cup diced sweet onion

½ cup diced bell pepper

½ cup small-diced cooked potatoes

½ cup shredded Cheddar cheese

6 large eggs

1 cup half-and-half

¼ teaspoon iodized salt

¼ teaspoon freshly ground black pepper

Sour cream and scallions or thinly sliced green onions for garnish

Preheat oven to 350 degrees F. Place the dough in a 9-inch deep-dish pie plate, fold extra pastry over the edges, and flute. Freeze at least 15 minutes.

Heat a small skillet over medium-high heat. Add chorizo and crumble it into small pieces as it browns. When the sausage is almost done, add the vegetables and cook until onions and peppers begin to soften. Remove from heat, drain excess fat, and set aside to cool.

Cover the bottom of the frozen pie crust with Cheddar cheese, then layer on the chorizo mixture. Set aside.

In a small bowl, whisk together eggs, half-and-half, salt, and pepper and pour over ingredients in pie crust.

Place the quiche on a parchment-lined baking sheet and bake 45–55 minutes, until the filling is completely set and does not jiggle. Remove from the oven and rest at room temperature 20 minutes before serving, so the slices will cut cleanly. Garnish with sour cream and sliced green onions.

Serves 6–8.

MIDWAY
BAKERY
QUICK
BREADS

Blueberry Muffins

Using tangy buttermilk and a modest amount of sugar makes this muffin less sweet than most and brings out the flavor of the blueberries. The oversize version of this muffin from the Midway Bakery is split and grilled at Wallace Station to accompany salad plates. For a sweeter, more traditional breakfast muffin, add ¼ cup sugar to the batter recipe below.

MUFFINS

2¼ cups all-purpose flour

2 teaspoons baking powder

½ teaspoon baking soda

½ cup sugar

½ teaspoon iodized salt

½ cup canola oil

2 large eggs, beaten

1 cup buttermilk

1 cup fresh or frozen blueberries

TOPPING

1 tablespoon sugar

¼ teaspoon nutmeg

Preheat oven to 375 degrees F. Line a 12-cup muffin pan with cupcake liners, or spray generously with nonstick spray. Set aside.

In a medium bowl, blend flour, baking powder, baking soda, sugar, and salt.

Make a well in the center and pour in oil, eggs, and buttermilk. Stir just until dry ingredients are moistened. If the batter seems too stiff, add a tablespoon or two of buttermilk. Fold in blueberries.

Using a scoop, portion the batter evenly among 12 muffin cups. In a small bowl, mix sugar and nutmeg topping and sprinkle evenly over muffins.

Bake 20 minutes, until muffins are golden brown and tops spring back when touched. Cool on wire racks.

Makes 12 muffins.

Sweet Potato Streusel Muffins

One of the most popular offerings at the Midway Bakery is the Sweet Potato Streusel Muffin. It has been on the menu since the bakery opened in 2011 and was created by then-manager Carrie Warmbier (Carrie also created a gluten-free version). Roasting the sweet potatoes makes a light and fluffy puree, with caramelization for added depth of flavor. Roasting the sweet potatoes the day before and cooling them overnight makes them easier to peel and puree.

MUFFINS

1½ cups flour

¾ teaspoon baking powder

¾ teaspoon baking soda

½ teaspoon iodized salt

1 teaspoon ground cinnamon

1 cup sugar

½ cup plus 2 tablespoons canola oil

2 teaspoons pure vanilla extract

2 medium sweet potatoes, roasted and pureed, about 2 cups (see note below)

2 large eggs

STREUSEL

¼ cup flour

¼ cup brown sugar

½ teaspoon ground ginger

2 tablespoons unsalted butter, softened

Preheat oven to 375 degrees F. Line a 12-cup muffin pan with cupcake liners, or spray generously with nonstick spray. Set aside.

For the muffin batter:
In a large bowl, whisk together flour, baking powder, baking soda, salt, and cinnamon and set aside.

In a medium bowl, whisk together sugar, oil, vanilla, sweet potato puree, and eggs. Add the wet ingredients to the dry ingredients and mix just until smooth.

For the streusel: Place flour, brown sugar, and ginger in a bowl and mix in softened butter by hand until the mixture is crumbly.

Assembly and baking: Using a scoop, portion the batter evenly among 12 muffin cups. Top each with streusel. Bake 25–28 minutes, or until a cake tester comes out clean.

Makes 12 muffins.

Note: To roast sweet potatoes, preheat oven to 400 degrees F. Prick potatoes with a knife in several places. Place them on a foil-lined baking pan and bake 1 hour. They are done when a knife can be inserted in the center with no resistance at all. If the knife cannot be inserted easily, return the potatoes to the oven and continue to bake. It is better to err on the side of overbaking rather than underbaking to ensure that the puree will be smooth and fluffy. Cool completely, peel, and puree the pulp in a food processor. Two medium sweet potatoes (about 1½ pounds) should yield about 2 cups of puree.

Sour Cream Coffee Cake

This coffee cake is so good it's best to make one for now and one to freeze for later. It can be made in a tube pan, a loaf pan, or a square baking pan. At the Midway Bakery, we use mini loaf pans and add slices to morning pastry trays, along with mini muffins and scones.

STREUSEL

½ cup flour

⅓ cup brown sugar

1 teaspoon ground cinnamon

½ teaspoon ground ginger

⅛ teaspoon iodized salt

3 tablespoons cold, unsalted butter, cut in small pieces

¾ cup toasted pecan pieces (optional)

COFFEE CAKE

¾ cup (1½ sticks) unsalted butter, at room temperature

1⅓ cups sugar

3 large eggs

1½ teaspoons pure vanilla extract

1¼ cups sour cream

2¼ teaspoons baking powder

½ teaspoon baking soda

¼ teaspoon iodized salt

2 cups all-purpose flour

Preheat oven to 350 degrees F. Generously grease and flour the pans of your choice: two 8½-by-4½-inch loaf pans, two 8-by-8-inch baking pans, or one 10-inch tube pan. Set aside.

For the streusel:
Whisk the dry ingredients together, then work the butter into the dry mixture using your fingers until it resembles coarse sand. Add pecans, if desired. Set aside.

For the coffee cake:
Cream butter and sugar at least 4 minutes, until fluffy and light in color. Add eggs one at a time, mixing well after each addition. Stir in vanilla and sour cream. In another bowl, whisk together baking powder, baking soda, salt, and flour. Add to the creamed mixture, mixing just until combined.

For two loaf pans or two square pans, divide the batter into four portions. Spread one-quarter of the batter in the bottom of each of the two pans, and cover with a generous ¼ cup streusel. Add the remaining batter by spoonfuls on top of the streusel in each pan and spread it evenly. Divide the remaining streusel between the two pans, sprinkling it evenly over the top layers of batter.

For a tube pan, divide the batter in half and spread half in the bottom of the prepared tube pan. Sprinkle with half the streusel. Drop spoonfuls of the remaining batter on top of the streusel, and spread the batter evenly. Top with remaining streusel.

Bake until the top springs back when pressed and a cake tester inserted in the center comes out clean:

Loaf pans: 50–60 minutes

Square pans: 25–30 minutes

Tube pan: 50–60 minutes

Zucchini Bread

The beautiful thing about this quick bread is that it allows gardeners to use up those extra-large zucchini that always seems to lurk under the plants' big leaves. It also provides a use for small portions of nuts, dried fruit, or baking chips that turn up when cleaning out the freezer or cabinet. We often make this recipe in mini loaf pans and add slices to breakfast pastry trays. When slathered with cream cheese, a slice of the traditional size is a perfect accompaniment to a summer salad plate or bowl of fruit. This recipe can easily be doubled.

2 large eggs

½ cup canola oil

¾ cup sugar

1½ cups shredded raw, unpeeled zucchini

1½ teaspoons pure vanilla extract

1½ cups all-purpose flour

1½ teaspoons ground cinnamon

¼ teaspoon ground nutmeg

½ teaspoon baking soda

¼ teaspoon baking powder

¼ teaspoon iodized salt

½ cup chopped, toasted nuts (optional)

½ cup golden raisins or other dried fruit (optional)

½ cup mini semisweet chocolate chips (optional)

Preheat oven to 350 degrees F. Prepare an 8½-by-4½-inch loaf pan with nonstick spray. Set aside.

In a medium bowl, whisk together eggs, canola oil, sugar, shredded zucchini, and vanilla extract. Set aside. In a large bowl, whisk together flour, cinnamon, nutmeg, baking soda, baking powder, and salt. Pour the wet ingredients into the dry, and mix well with a rubber spatula or wooden spoon. Fold in nuts, fruits, or baking chips, if desired.

Bake 50 minutes. Cool on a wire rack.

Makes 1 loaf.

2

Building Blocks for Sandwiches

Almost every weekend during the late spring, when we were all dying to get out of the house, my dad would take a whole loaf of Roman Meal soft wheat bread and stack baloney and American cheese with a squirt of yellow mustard between every other slice. He'd pile all the sandwiches together, slip them back into the bread bag, and off we'd go to the Red River Gorge for a hike and a picnic. Dad also loved peanut butter and baloney sandwiches.

continued

My mother had a different approach to sandwiches. She baked sourdough bread and beer bread and made egg salad, tuna salad, ham salad, roast beef salad, and, famously, tongue salad. Many days I would open my lunch at school and find a tongue salad sandwich on sourdough, which I would promptly trade to my sixth-grade teacher for a bag of peanuts or a piece of cheese. I hated my mom's tongue salad then, but I'd give anything for one of her sandwiches now. She also loved spicy Indian lime pickle, sprouts, and egg salad on dense whole wheat bread.

We would often start the day with an egg sandwich: a fried egg with mayonnaise, cheese, and maybe a slice of tomato in the summer. Or sometimes we'd have open-faced Velveeta cheese toast with sliced tomato.

A great sandwich involves attention to detail and delicious ingredients. At my restaurants, we spend hours making chicken salad, slicing turkey and ham, pulling pork, slicing tomatoes, and baking whole wheat, white, and rye breads. Our customers have favorite sandwich combinations that influence the menu. Some are so popular that our guests won't let us change them, and others change all the time. The staff constantly innovates, sneaking their own favorites onto the menu.

The wonderful part of sandwich making is that it is based on customer preference. There is no affront to the chef when diners craft their own sandwiches the way they like them. The sandwich is a humble but delicious meal that is easy to share and easy to take along on a hike.

SANDWICH SPREADS

The Wallace Station Country Ham and Pimiento Cheese Panini, a warm, gooey, savory sandwich, received a nice shout-out from the personable—and quotable—Jason Smith of Grayson, Kentucky, who was the 2017 winner of the *Food Network Star* television competition. We were honored when Smith praised the sandwich's virtues on the Cooking Channel's *Best Thing I Ever Ate* program. "When you take a bite, you know it's not just a good sandwich, it's a great sandwich," Smith said. "Life-changing—trust me."

Wallace Station Pimiento Cheese

Pimiento cheese has been popular from day one at Wallace Station. My sister, Paige, who opened the restaurant with me, added cream cheese as the secret ingredient. It is now on the menu at all our locations. This spread is also great as a cold sandwich or as a topping for crackers.

8 ounces white Cheddar cheese, shredded

4 ounces cream cheese, softened

6 tablespoons mayonnaise

½ teaspoon Worcestershire sauce

1½ teaspoons hot sauce

1 teaspoon minced onion

1 teaspoon horseradish

1 (2-ounce) jar diced pimientos, drained

Place all ingredients except pimientos in the bowl of an electric mixer and mix thoroughly on medium speed using the paddle attachment. The mixture should be slightly chunky. Fold in pimientos. Taste for seasoning, and chill before serving.

Makes 1 quart.

Benedictine

Benedictine is another recipe that's used throughout my restaurants. The spread's roots are in Louisville, where it was created by Jennie Benedict (1860–1928), a revered cook and hostess and author of *The Blue Ribbon Cook Book*. This version is from Carol Laufer, a noted Louisville event planner, and was shared by her daughter, Lisa Laufer, Holly Hill Inn's sous chef emeritus. Note that, unlike other benedictine recipes, this one does not add green food coloring or mayonnaise. Lisa makes benedictine like no one else, and it's the best I've ever had.

This classic Kentucky spread is a must-have for any Derby party. Benedictine is often served with smoked trout on hoecakes, classically with bacon. I like a BB&T—benedictine, bacon, and tomato—on white. It's good with crackers or crudités as well.

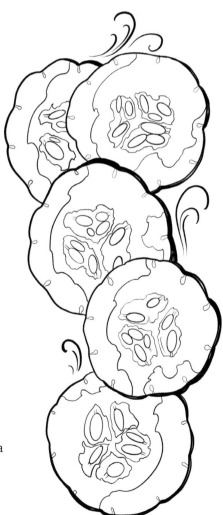

2 large cucumbers (about 9 ounces each)

12 ounces cream cheese, at room temperature

Onion juice to taste; start with ½ teaspoon (see note below)

½ teaspoon kosher salt, or more to taste

3–4 dashes hot sauce

Peel cucumbers, retaining a bit of skin for color. Puree in a food processor. Squeeze cucumber puree in cheesecloth, removing as much liquid as possible. This keeps the spread from being too runny. Cucumber juice is delicious in a Bloody Mary or chilled with a splash of lemon and vodka.

Combine all ingredients in a mixer or food processor and mix until smooth. Taste for seasoning.

Makes about 2 cups.

Note: For onion juice, grate one-quarter of a peeled onion on a cheese grater and squeeze out the juice using cheesecloth.

Olive Nut Spread

This was a favorite of Midway native Betty Ann Voigt, one of the first people to welcome Chris and me to this Bluegrass town in 2000. She lamented that no one made a good olive nut spread anymore, so we created one for her.

1 (8-ounce) package cream cheese, softened

½ cup pecans, toasted and chopped

1 cup pimiento-stuffed Spanish olives, chopped

2 tablespoons olive brine

1 teaspoon hot sauce

Combine all ingredients in the bowl of an electric mixer and blend thoroughly. Place in a covered container and refrigerate.

Makes about 2 cups.

Feta Walnut Spread

Adapted from a medieval recipe, this spread is served annually at the Midway Christian Church's Epiphany dinner in January. It is also served at Wallace Station and Holly Hill Inn during asparagus season, when we use the spread in a veggie wrap with roasted asparagus grown by Shelley Johnson of Woodford County, olive tapenade, baby greens, green onions, and roasted red pepper.

4 ounces cream cheese, softened

¾ cup small-curd cottage cheese

½ cup crumbled Feta cheese

⅓ cup finely chopped celery

1 green onion, minced

1 tablespoon minced fresh flat-leaf parsley

1 tablespoon minced fresh mint

½ cup hand-chopped toasted walnuts

¼ teaspoon freshly ground black pepper

Kosher salt to taste

Mix cream cheese, cottage cheese, and Feta cheese in the bowl of an electric mixer on medium-high speed until well blended but still chunky. Add remaining ingredients and mix on low speed until well combined. Chill about 30 minutes before serving.

Makes 2¼ cups.

Pimiento Blue Cheese

This spread was created by coauthor Sara Gibbs for the 2009 Southern Foodways Alliance Conference at the University of Mississippi in Oxford. Conference participants received box lunches that were served in The Grove, a ten-acre wooded tailgating area in the center of campus. The box included spicy bourbon barbecue chicken, so a blue cheese spread for fresh vegetable dipping was the obvious accompaniment. Rather than the traditional blue cheese dressing, pimiento cheese starring Gorgonzola seemed fitting for Southern food lovers. We later found that it also makes a fabulous hamburger topping and a unique addition to a Cobb salad, which Sara also created for Wallace Station and Windy Corner Market—a happy accident!

8 ounces Kenny's aged white Cheddar cheese, shredded (or any white Cheddar of your choice)

½ cup mayonnaise

1 teaspoon Worcestershire sauce

1 tablespoon minced roasted garlic (see index for how to roast garlic)

2 tablespoons minced shallots

¼ teaspoon white pepper

8 ounces Gorgonzola or other blue cheese crumbles

1 (2-ounce) jar diced pimientos, well drained

Combine white Cheddar, mayonnaise, Worcestershire sauce, roasted garlic, shallots, and white pepper in a large bowl and stir with a rubber spatula until well combined. Fold in Gorgonzola and pimientos and mix just until combined. The spread will be chunky.

Makes 2¾ cups.

Bourbon White Cheddar Cheese Spread

The addition of bourbon to this classic cheeseball recipe from Sara's mother, Mabel Thompson, makes it special, and the milk makes it spreadable. Eliminate the milk to obtain a mixture that is thick enough to be formed into a ball and rolled in crushed toasted pecans or minced parsley and served with crostini and crudités. One Christmas, Sara and I made cheeseball truffles for the holiday open house at the Woodford Reserve Distillery Visitor's Center, where they were a crowd favorite.

1 (8-ounce) package cream cheese, softened and cut into pieces

6 ounces sharp white Cheddar cheese, shredded

1 tablespoon Worcestershire sauce

3 tablespoons minced yellow onion

1 tablespoon Woodford Reserve bourbon

¼ teaspoon ground sweet paprika

Pinch cayenne pepper, or to taste

¼ cup whole milk

In the bowl of an electric mixer, whip cream cheese, white Cheddar, Worcestershire sauce, onion, bourbon, paprika, and cayenne until well blended and fluffy. Add enough milk to make the mixture spreadable. Chill at least 1 hour before using.

Makes 2 cups.

Lisa's Boursin Cheese

This spread mimics Boursin garlic and fine herbs, a creamy cheese first developed in the Normandy region of France. It is at home at a cocktail buffet or on a sandwich. Holly Hill Inn usually serves it at Christmas. The spread tastes great with a hot pepper jelly.

1 (8-ounce) package cream cheese, softened

½ cup (1 stick) unsalted butter, softened

¼ teaspoon garlic salt

¼ teaspoon dried oregano

⅛ teaspoon dried basil

⅛ teaspoon dried dill

⅛ teaspoon dried marjoram

⅛ teaspoon freshly ground black pepper

⅛ teaspoon dried thyme

Blend all ingredients in the bowl of an electric mixer until smooth and creamy. Chill at least 30 minutes before using.

Makes 1½ cups.

Cranberry Mustard

Chef Paul Hieb created this spicy condiment for the fall menu at Glenn's Creek Café, our former lunch counter at Woodford Reserve Distillery. Pair this spread with smoked or roasted turkey, Swiss cheese, and Bourbon Mayonnaise (see the recipe later in this chapter) for a Thanksgiving-inspired sandwich that can be served year-round.

½ cup white vinegar

½ cup water, divided

2 tablespoons mustard seeds

1½ cups dried cranberries

1 teaspoon dry mustard

¼ cup Dijon mustard

In a small saucepan, heat vinegar, ¼ cup water, mustard seeds, and cranberries and bring to a boil. Remove from heat, cover, and rest 15 minutes to allow cranberries to soften. Stir in dry mustard and Dijon and pour into a food processor. Process until smooth enough to spread, adding enough water (up to ¼ cup) to achieve the right consistency.

Makes 1¾ cups.

Bourbon Tomato Jam

Tomato jam is best made in the middle of summer, when fresh ripe tomatoes are available, but this version uses canned tomatoes, so you can make it year-round. The flavors of bourbon and tomato are surprisingly compatible. This sweet-and-spicy spread pairs well with country ham, meatloaf, and turkey on biscuits or sandwiches.

4 cups (one 28-ounce can and one 15-ounce can) canned diced tomatoes, well drained

1½ cups sugar

⅔ cup apple cider vinegar

⅛ teaspoon cayenne pepper

½ cup chopped onion

1 bay leaf

½ teaspoon ground cinnamon

⅛ teaspoon ground cloves

¼ teaspoon ground nutmeg

¼ teaspoon dry mustard

½ teaspoon kosher salt

3 tablespoons bourbon

Pour tomatoes into a colander to drain while proceeding with the recipe. Bring sugar and vinegar to a boil and simmer until thickened and clear. Add remaining ingredients except bourbon and simmer until thick, about 35 minutes. Add bourbon and simmer another 5–10 minutes, until most of the liquid has evaporated but the mixture is still spreadable. It will thicken as it chills.

Cool to room temperature. Remove bay leaf. Pour into a food processor and pulse until spreadable. Chill at least 30 minutes before using.

Makes 2½ cups.

Sun-Dried Tomato Olive Tapenade

Adding bourbon and sun-dried tomatoes to Holly Hill Inn's olive tapenade recipe makes this spread just a little sweeter. Use it as a base for wraps or sandwiches. The tapenade is especially good when paired with Feta Walnut Spread.

3 ounces pimiento-stuffed
green olives (about ½ cup)

3 ounces kalamata olives (about ½ cup)

¼ cup julienne sun-dried tomatoes
(soaked in hot water and squeezed dry)

½ ounce anchovies, chopped, or
1 teaspoon anchovy paste

1 clove garlic, minced

1½ tablespoons capers, drained and rinsed

2 tablespoons olive oil

¼ teaspoon freshly ground black pepper

1 tablespoon bourbon

½ tablespoon fresh lemon juice

2 tablespoons minced parsley

Combine all ingredients in a food processor and process to a chunky paste. Taste for seasoning, and chill before using.

Makes about 1¼ cups.

Bourbon Mayonnaise

Blending mayonnaise with leftover Bourbon Sorghum Vinaigrette (see chapter 6) makes an inspired sandwich condiment. We especially like it with Bourbon-Brined Roasted Turkey Breast (see the recipe later in this chapter) or our Kentucky-style Bourbon Banh Mi (see chapter 3).

1 cup mayonnaise

1 tablespoon Bourbon Sorghum Vinaigrette
(see index)

Blend in a small bowl. Chill before serving.

Makes 1 cup.

SANDWICH MEATS
AND FILLINGS

Wallace Station Tuna Salad

Barry T's was a sandwich shop down by the University of Kentucky, under Sqecial Media on Limestone. My sister, Paige, worked there and was inspired to create Wallace Station's tuna salad and veggie cheese sandwich after Barry T's closed.

___

2 (5-ounce) cans albacore or
chunk light tuna, well drained

2 tablespoons finely chopped red onion

3 tablespoons sweet pickle
relish, well drained

½ cup mayonnaise

Pinch ground cloves

Pinch ground cinnamon

Pinch ground allspice

⅛ teaspoon freshly ground black pepper

Kosher salt to taste

___

Squeeze tuna dry and place in a medium bowl. Add remaining ingredients and mix well. Taste for seasoning. Cover and chill.

Makes about 1½ cups.

Shady Lane Chicken Salad

I love a good chicken salad. One of the most popular lunches at Holly Hill Inn was a chicken salad plate, so we included chicken salad on the Wallace Station menu when that restaurant opened and quickly added it to the Windy Corner Market menu when customers demanded it.

This recipe is named for Shady Lane, also known as Old Frankfort Pike, a Kentucky Scenic Byway along which Wallace Station sits. Chicken salad is a standard in local community cookbooks, and all the best restaurants and caterers have a good chicken salad. Dried cranberries are used here rather than green grapes, a traditional ingredient in many recipes, because the salad holds better.

2 pounds boneless, skinless chicken breasts, trimmed of excess fat

Salt and pepper for seasoning

½ cup finely chopped celery

½ cup toasted slivered almonds

½ cup dried cranberries

½ teaspoon kosher salt

¼ teaspoon dry mustard

¼ teaspoon white pepper

¼ teaspoon freshly ground black pepper

1½ tablespoons Dijon mustard

1 cup mayonnaise

Preheat oven to 350 degrees F.

Spread chicken in a single layer on a baking pan and lightly season with salt and pepper. Cover with foil and bake until done (40 minutes or longer, depending on size). Cool in the pan juices (to retain moisture) until the chicken is easy to handle. Cut into a small dice (preferable to pulling, which can cause the meat to dry out), discarding gristle and fat. Reserve pan juices for soup or another use.

Place chopped chicken, celery, almonds, and cranberries in a large bowl. Set aside.

In another small bowl, whisk together remaining ingredients and fold into chicken. Mix well. Taste for seasoning and add salt and pepper if needed. Remember that chicken will absorb the dressing when refrigerated, so you might have to add a couple of extra tablespoons of mayonnaise.

Chill at least 1 hour before serving.

Makes almost 2 quarts.

Margaret Ware's Egg Salad

Midway native Margaret Ware Parrish was related to Judge Caleb Wallace, an early and notable resident of Woodford County for whom Wallace Station is named. Margaret didn't cook much, but she loved egg salad, so I would make it for her by the quart. She didn't like any fancy additions, but it's often made with a little pickle relish and is great with chopped asparagus.

6 large eggs

¼ cup mayonnaise (or more to taste)

¼ teaspoon dry mustard

¼ teaspoon kosher salt, or more to taste

Several grindings black pepper

Place eggs in a medium saucepan. Add warm water until eggs are covered by ½ inch. Bring to a boil. Turn off heat, cover, and let stand 15–20 minutes. Place in an ice bath for 5 minutes to stop the cooking process. Peel under running water, and place in a large bowl. Mash eggs with a fork, then fold in remaining ingredients, adding more mayonnaise sparingly as needed.

Makes about 1½ cups.

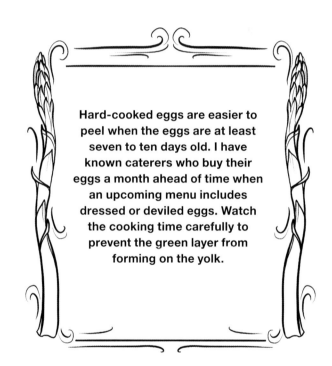

Hard-cooked eggs are easier to peel when the eggs are at least seven to ten days old. I have known caterers who buy their eggs a month ahead of time when an upcoming menu includes dressed or deviled eggs. Watch the cooking time carefully to prevent the green layer from forming on the yolk.

Ale-8-One Sloppy Joes

This sloppy joe was a favorite at the Woodford Reserve Distillery Visitor's Center, where we operated Glenn's Creek Café and Glenn's Creek Catering from 2009 to 2020. Using grass-fed beef raised just down the road and Ale-8-One, a gingery soda made in Winchester, Kentucky, makes this version unique to the Bluegrass State.

1½ pounds ground beef

1 medium onion, finely diced (about 1 cup)

1 clove garlic, minced

1½ tablespoons flour

⅔ cup ketchup

½ cup Ale-8-One

2 tablespoons tomato paste

1 (8-ounce) can tomato sauce

1 tablespoon apple cider vinegar

1 tablespoon Worcestershire sauce

1½ teaspoons honey

1 teaspoon dry mustard

1 tablespoon chili powder

½ teaspoon freshly ground black pepper

Kosher salt to taste

6–8 sturdy burger buns

Brown ground beef, onion, and garlic in a deep skillet over medium-high heat. Remove from the stove and carefully drain excess fat.

Return pan to medium heat and stir in flour. Cook about 2 minutes, then stir in remaining ingredients. Cover, reduce heat to medium-low, and simmer 15 minutes. To make the mixture extra sloppy, add more Ale-8-One. Taste for seasoning. Remove from heat and allow the sloppy joe mixture to rest about 5 minutes before serving, which helps it tighten up. Serve warm on buns.

Makes about 1 quart.
Serves 6–8.

Hot Turkey Salad

This is our take on an old-fashioned ladies' lunch recipe found in numerous community and church cookbooks. It can also be made with chicken. Hot Turkey Salad is a very popular lunch item at Holly Hill Inn.

3½ cups chopped cooked turkey

¾ cup dry wild rice, cooked according to package directions

½ cup white rice, cooked according to package directions

2 (8-ounce) cans sliced water chestnuts, drained and rinsed

4 ounces cream cheese, softened

2 cups mayonnaise

2 cups shredded white Cheddar cheese

1 cup sour cream

½ cup minced red onion

1 cup small-diced celery

1 teaspoon kosher salt, or more to taste

1 teaspoon white pepper

Preheat oven to 350 degrees F. Coat a deep 13-by-9-inch pan with nonstick spray. Set aside.

Mix all ingredients in a large bowl until well blended. Pour into the prepared baking pan and spread evenly. Bake 45–50 minutes, until golden brown and bubbling around the edges and hot in the middle.

Makes 14–16 servings.

ROASTED MEATS

We learned early on that sandwiches can be very expensive to make, especially when you bake your own bread. Finding natural, high-quality deli meats at a reasonable price was difficult. We soon realized that roasting our own top sirloins and chickens or braising pork butts and chuck roasts was more economical and allowed us to use Kentucky-raised meats. Our sandwiches are a combination of slow-cooked local meats and the best ham, country ham, and roast turkey we can find.

Porchetta

Porchetta is a traditional Italian preparation in which pork is deboned and stuffed, smeared with garlic and herbs, and slow-roasted and smoked over an open fire. In this simplified version, herb paste is rubbed on a boneless pork loin to make a moist, savory sandwich filling with the thinly sliced meat. Pairing Porchetta with herb aioli, marinated vegetables, and Provolone makes a sandwich worthy of a special summer picnic.

2-pound boneless pork loin

HERB PASTE

1½ tablespoons minced fresh rosemary

1½ tablespoons minced fresh sage

3 tablespoons olive oil

½ teaspoon freshly ground black pepper

½ teaspoon ground sweet paprika

1½ teaspoons minced fresh garlic

1½ teaspoons kosher salt

Preheat oven to 425 degrees F.

Mix herb paste ingredients in a small bowl. Smear herb paste on all sides of the pork loin. Place pork in a roasting pan and roast 25 minutes. Reduce heat to 350 degrees F and roast another 45 minutes, until the internal temperature reaches 145 degrees F.

Let the roast rest 10 minutes before slicing.

Serves 6.

Chile-Ginger Roasted Pork

Paul Hieb created this roasted pork loin for his Bourbon Banh Mi (see chapter 3), a Kentucky-inspired sandwich based on the Vietnamese banh mi. Marinating the pork for 1 hour before roasting allows the spicy Asian flavors to permeate the meat.

2-pound boneless pork loin

MARINADE

1 tablespoon minced fresh ginger root

1 tablespoon sambal oelek (in the Asian section of your grocery store)

2 tablespoons fish sauce

Prepare a roasting pan with nonstick spray. Mix marinade ingredients in a small bowl. Place pork loin in the roasting pan and pour marinade over it, covering all sides. Cover and rest 1 hour to allow flavors to develop.

Preheat oven to 425 degrees F. Roast the pork 25 minutes, reduce heat to 350 degrees F, and continue to roast another 35 minutes, or until the internal temperature reaches 145 degrees F.

Let the roast rest 10 minutes before slicing.

Serves 6.

Bourbon-Brined Roasted Turkey Breast

This bourbon brine comes from Holly Hill Inn, but it is used in many of my restaurants. At one time, Glenn's Creek Café served a sandwich called Turkey in the Rye that featured smoked bourbon-brined turkey breast and Cranberry Mustard (see the recipe earlier in this chapter). Roasting large cuts of meat in-house for sandwich fillings is more economical and allows us to provide our guests with a healthier alternative to deli meats, which are often injected with curing solutions.

6- to 8-pound bone-in whole turkey breast, thawed if frozen (see note below)

BRINE

1 gallon hot water

1 cup kosher salt

1 quart bourbon

1 cup sorghum or molasses

1 cup brown sugar

6 whole cloves

8 whole black peppercorns

8 whole allspice berries

2 bay leaves

1 cinnamon stick

---

4 tablespoons melted unsalted butter

Rinse turkey breast under cold water and place in a large stockpot or other large, sturdy container, breast side down. The container has to hold both the turkey and a large amount of brine because the meat must be submerged in the liquid. Clear space in the refrigerator for the container.

Mix brine ingredients until salt and sorghum dissolve, then cool to room temperature. Pour brine over turkey, cover, and refrigerate 12–24 hours.

Remove turkey from brine and pat dry with paper towels. Place breast side up in a roasting pan that has been coated with nonstick spray, then return to the refrigerator for 1 hour. Allowing the turkey to dry helps produce a crisp skin. Remove the turkey from the refrigerator and rest on the counter for 30 minutes.

Preheat oven to 425 degrees F. Brush turkey breast with melted butter and roast 30 minutes. Reduce heat to 350 degrees F and continue roasting until the internal temperature at the thickest part of the breast reaches 170 degrees F, about 2 hours. After roasting 1 hour at 350 degrees, check the internal temperature every 15 minutes.

Remove turkey from the oven, tent with foil, and rest 15 minutes before slicing.

Serves 8.

Note: A fresh turkey breast without saline injections or flavor enhancements is best for this recipe.

Wallace Station Pulled Cubano Pork

3- to 3½-pound boneless pork butt

¼ cup Jared's Pork Rub (recipe follows)

Wallace Station Chicken Salt (recipe follows)

Rub pork butt with Jared's Pork Rub and refrigerate several hours or overnight.

Preheat oven to 425 degrees F. Place pork butt in a baking pan and roast, uncovered, 30–40 minutes, until the rub begins to darken and char. Reduce heat to 300 degrees F. Remove roasted pork from the oven and add water to a depth of ½ inch in the pan. Cover and continue baking 1½–2 hours, or until the internal temperature registers 200 degrees F and the meat is very tender.

Remove the roast from the liquid and cool slightly. When the meat can be handled, discard any visible fat and pull the pork into shreds using two forks. Season lightly with Wallace Station Chicken Salt. The pork can be used to make quesadillas or tacos or tossed in barbecue sauce for pulled pork sandwiches.

The leftover pan juices can be chilled, causing any fat to rise to the top and solidify. After discarding the fat, the rich broth can be used as part of the stock for Whitesburg Soup Beans (see chapter 6).

Jared's Pork Rub

The long list of spices in this recipe might look daunting, but the complex flavor that results is worth the effort. The spicy and herbal flavor notes are a perfect combination for a great Cubano. This recipe makes more than you need for one pork butt, but the leftover rub will keep for up to 6 months. Mix up a batch at the beginning of grilling season and enjoy it on any cut of pork or chicken.

6 tablespoons light brown sugar

6 tablespoons kosher salt

1 teaspoon crushed red pepper flakes

½ teaspoon ground cinnamon

½ teaspoon ground coriander

3 tablespoons leaf oregano

2 tablespoons dry mustard

1½ tablespoons freshly ground black pepper

1 teaspoon ground nutmeg

1 teaspoon ground cloves

6 tablespoons ground sweet paprika

3 tablespoons ground cumin

3 tablespoons dried leaf thyme

Blend all ingredients thoroughly with a whisk, making sure there are no clumps of brown sugar. Store tightly covered.

Makes 1¾ cups.

Wallace Station Chicken Salt

Chicken salt is a nice addition to roasted vegetables or as a seasoning on hamburgers and grilled meat.

¼ cup kosher salt

¼ teaspoon cayenne

¼ teaspoon freshly ground black pepper

¼ teaspoon ground sweet paprika

Blend thoroughly in a small bowl.

Makes ¼ cup.

Sean's Monday Night Meatloaf

This flavorful meatloaf is served every Wednesday at Wallace Station and is the Monday night special at Windy Corner Market, where the recipe was developed by longtime chef Sean Willoughby. The regulars love it.

MEATLOAF

1½ pounds ground beef

1 pound Stone Cross Farm breakfast sausage

1 tablespoon Worcestershire sauce

3 large eggs

⅓ cup Bourbon Barbecue Sauce (see index)

2 teaspoons kosher salt

1½ teaspoons freshly ground black pepper

1 teaspoon dried thyme

⅓ cup diced green bell pepper

1 rib celery, chopped (a generous ½ cup)

¾ cup chopped yellow onion

2 green onions, chopped

2 garlic cloves, chopped

1 tablespoon unsalted butter

½ cup diced fresh tomato

2½–2¾ cups homemade bread crumbs (stale bread toasted and pureed in a food processor)

GLAZE

½ cup ketchup

2 tablespoons brown sugar

¼ teaspoon freshly ground black pepper

½ teaspoon yellow mustard

Preheat oven to 350 degrees F. Line the bottom of a 9-by-5-inch loaf pan with parchment and spray with nonstick spray. Set aside.

Mix ground beef and sausage with Worcestershire sauce, eggs, barbecue sauce, salt, pepper, and thyme in a large bowl. Set aside.

Puree green bell pepper, celery, onion, green onions, and garlic in a food processor. The mixture should be slightly chunky and have some texture. Set aside.

Heat butter in a large sauté pan. Add bell pepper mixture and sauté over medium heat.

Cool slightly, then add to the meat mixture along with diced tomato and bread crumbs. Use gloved hands to make sure the mixture is well combined so no pockets remain after baking.

Press mixture gently into the prepared loaf pan, carefully pressing and working it into the corners so the loaf is well packed and will make an even slice. Place the loaf pan on a sheet pan to catch any drips.

Bake 1 hour. While the meatloaf is cooking, mix glaze ingredients in a small bowl and set aside.

After 1 hour, pull the meatloaf out of the oven, carefully pour off the fat, and spread the glaze over the top. Return to the oven and bake 15 minutes, until the internal temperature reaches 155 degrees F. Rest 10–15 minutes before cutting, so the slices will hold together.

Each loaf makes 7 generous slices.

WALLACE STATION
SANDWICH BREADS

When I opened Wallace Station in 2003, I searched the marketplace for a sandwich bread with structure and density. My mother had baked all the breads for our lunch boxes, so I grew up with that style and wanted a sandwich bread that had enough body to hold up to panini presses and lots of fillings. We had a flour mill right down the road, so we thought, why not make our own bread?

continued

Clay McClure was the first baker at Wallace Station. She then taught Nicolas Medina, who baked the bread there until 2011, when he moved to the newly opened Midway Bakery.

Honestly, we never thought Wallace Station would become such a popular sandwich shop. We thought we would bake all the breads and desserts for Holly Hill Inn at Wallace Station and hoped to sell enough sandwiches to break even. Wallace Station has since turned into a destination for tourists and Keeneland Race Course patrons and a weekly routine for our Bluegrass neighbors. This little sandwich shop is one of the places people go for a Kentucky experience.

"When I lived in Kentucky, I often had trouble getting bread dough to rise, especially in the winter. I usually tried to time my bread baking with doing the laundry. Closing the door of the laundry room and turning on the dryer made a pretty good proofing box, even on the coldest days. Now that I live in Florida, I put the towel-covered dough outside on the porch in the shade, and it practically leaps out of the pan in 40 minutes. The heat and humidity outside mimic the conditions in a proofing cabinet, making the process quick and easy. Resting the mixture before shaping produces a smooth, soft dough that is easier to handle."

— Sara Gibbs

Wallace Station White Bread

1 envelope (¼ ounce) active
dry yeast (2¼ teaspoons)

1 tablespoon plus pinch sugar

3¾ cups bread flour

1 teaspoon iodized salt

1 tablespoon vegetable oil

1¼–1½ cups water, divided

Prepare a 9-by-5-inch loaf pan with nonstick spray. Set aside.

Mix yeast with a pinch of sugar in ½ cup lukewarm water (105–115 degrees F) and stir with a fork until completely dissolved. Let rest 5–10 minutes until it foams vigorously.

Mix 1 tablespoon sugar, flour, and salt in the bowl of an electric mixer fitted with a beater. Add vegetable oil and yeast mixture. Begin mixing and slowly add about ¾ cup lukewarm water until the dough holds together in a ball and pulls away from the sides of the bowl. The amount of water can vary, so add it slowly and watch the dough's consistency. It should be tacky but not wet. Once the dough has come together, remove the beater, cover the bowl with a towel, and let the dough rest 20 minutes. This allows the flour to hydrate and produces a light, airy loaf.

After 20 minutes, attach the dough hook to the mixer and knead on low speed about 3 minutes. If the dough travels up the dough hook, stop the mixer, push the dough down to the bottom of the bowl, and wrap it around the hook. Do this several times, if necessary. Do not overknead, or the dough will be tough. (Alternatively, the dough can be kneaded by hand: Place the dough on a floured surface and knead briefly, until it is smooth and elastic.)

Turn the dough out onto a lightly floured surface. Pat or roll it into a rectangle roughly 10 inches by 8 inches. Position the dough horizontally and, using both hands, roll it into a tight spiral. Tuck the ends underneath and pinch the bottom seams together to seal. Place the dough in the prepared loaf pan, seam side down, settling it snugly in the center of the pan.

Cover with a towel, place in a warm area, and let rise 1–1½ hours, or until the dough expands to about 1 inch over the rim of the pan.

Preheat oven to 425 degrees F. Bake 10 minutes, then reduce heat to 375 degrees F and bake another 25 minutes, or until the internal temperature is 200 degrees F. Check the temperature by inserting an instant-read thermometer into the center of the loaf. The crust should be golden brown, and the bottom should sound hollow when tapped. Remove the loaf from the pan immediately and cool on a wire rack.

Makes 1 sandwich loaf.

Wallace Station Whole Wheat Bread

At the Midway Bakery, this bread is made with Weisenberger Mill cracked wheat, but if you can't find it in the grocery store, old-fashioned rolled oats make a good substitute and contribute a nice crunchiness to this sturdy sandwich loaf.

½ cup cracked wheat or old-fashioned rolled oats

1 envelope (¼ ounce) active dry yeast (2¼ teaspoons)

Pinch sugar

1¾ cups bread flour

1¾ cups whole wheat flour

1½ teaspoons iodized salt

1 tablespoon vegetable oil

1 tablespoon honey

1 tablespoon molasses

1½–1¾ cups water, divided

Prepare a 9-by-5-inch loaf pan with nonstick spray. Set aside.

Place cracked wheat or rolled oats in a small bowl. (For rolled oats, first grind in a food processor to obtain medium flakes.) Add ½ cup warm water. Mix with a fork, set aside, and let stand 30 minutes until the grains hydrate. After the grains have been hydrating 20 minutes, bloom the yeast by mixing yeast with a pinch of sugar in ½ cup lukewarm water (105–115 degrees F) until completely dissolved. Let rest 5–10 minutes until it foams vigorously.

Mix flours and salt in the bowl of an electric mixer fitted with a beater. Add hydrated grains, yeast mixture, vegetable oil, honey, and molasses. Begin mixing and slowly add about ¾ cup lukewarm water until the dough holds together in a ball and pulls away from the sides of the bowl. The amount of water can vary, so add it slowly and watch the dough's consistency. It should be tacky but not wet. Once the dough has come together, remove the beater, cover the bowl with a towel, and let the dough rest 20 minutes.

After resting, the dough should be smooth and pliable. Attach the dough hook to the mixer and knead on medium speed 2–3 minutes. The dough should come together in a ball and pull away from the sides of the mixing bowl. If the dough travels up the dough hook, stop the mixer, push the dough down to the bottom of the bowl, and wrap it around the hook. Do this several times, if necessary. Do not overknead, or the dough will be tough. (Alternatively, the dough can be kneaded by hand: Place the dough on a floured surface and knead briefly, until it is smooth and elastic.)

Turn the dough out on a floured surface. Pat or roll it into a rectangle roughly 10 inches by 8 inches. Position the dough horizontally and, using both hands, roll it into a tight spiral. Tuck the ends underneath and pinch the bottom seams together to seal. Place the dough in the prepared loaf pan, seam side down, settling it snugly in the center of the pan.

Cover with a towel, place in a warm area, and let rise 1½ hours, or until the dough expands to about 1 inch over the rim of the pan.

Preheat oven to 425 degrees F. Bake 10 minutes, then reduce heat to 375 degrees F and bake another 25 minutes, or until the internal temperature is 200 degrees F. Check the temperature by inserting an instant-read thermometer into the center of the loaf. The crust should be golden brown, and the bottom should sound hollow when tapped. Remove the loaf from the pan immediately and cool on a wire rack.

Makes 1 sandwich loaf.

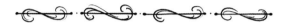

Wallace Station Rye Bread

It is worth the effort to make this rye bread because of its unique taste. Rather than the sour, tangy flavor of traditional rye bread, this bread actually tastes sweet. The combination of rye flour and wheat flour produces a lighter loaf than its European counterparts.

1 envelope (¼ ounce) active dry yeast (2¼ teaspoons)

Pinch sugar

2 cups bread flour

1¼ cups rye flour

1 teaspoon iodized salt

2 tablespoons caraway seeds

1½ tablespoons vegetable oil

1 tablespoon molasses

1¼–1½ cups water, divided

Prepare a 9-by-5-inch loaf pan with nonstick spray. Set aside.

Mix yeast with a pinch of sugar in ½ cup lukewarm water (105–115 degrees F) and stir with a fork until completely dissolved. Let rest 5–10 minutes until it foams vigorously.

Mix flours, salt, and caraway seeds in the bowl of an electric mixer fitted with a beater. Add yeast mixture, vegetable oil, and molasses. Begin mixing and slowly add about ¾ cup water until the dough holds together in a ball and pulls away from the sides of the bowl. The amount of water can vary, so add it slowly and watch the dough's consistency. It should be tacky but not wet. Once the dough has come together, remove the beater, cover the bowl with a towel, and let the dough rest 20 minutes. This allows the flours to hydrate and produces a light, airy loaf.

After 20 minutes, attach the dough hook to the mixer and knead on low speed about 3 minutes. If the dough travels up the dough hook, stop the mixer, push the dough down to the bottom of the bowl, and wrap it around the hook. Do this several times, if necessary. Do not overknead, or the dough will be tough. (Alternatively, the dough can be kneaded by hand: Place the dough on a floured surface and knead briefly, until it is smooth and elastic.)

Turn the dough out onto a lightly floured surface. Pat or roll it into a rectangle roughly 10 inches by 8 inches. Position the dough horizontally and, using both hands, roll it into a tight spiral. Tuck the ends underneath and pinch the bottom seams together to seal. Place the dough in the prepared loaf pan, seam side down, settling it snugly in the center of the pan.

Cover with a towel, place in a warm area, and let rise 1–1½ hours, or until the dough expands to about 1 inch over the rim of the pan.

Preheat oven to 425 degrees F. Bake 10 minutes, then reduce heat to 375 degrees F and bake another 25 minutes, or until the internal temperature is

200 degrees F. Check the temperature by inserting an instant-read thermometer into the center of the loaf. The crust should be golden brown, and the bottom should sound hollow when tapped. Remove the loaf from the pan immediately and cool on a wire rack.

Makes 1 sandwich loaf.

BUILDING BLOCKS FOR SANDWICHES

3

Wallace Station's Famous Sandwiches

Wallace Station is rooted in its history as a country store, post office, and rail stop and in my husband Chris's experience at Plain and Fancy, a small roadside deli and bakery in East Hampton, New York, owned by our friends Dave and Maria Bernier. Chris grew up spending the summers with his family in a little cottage in East Hampton, a couple of blocks away from Main Beach. The summer after graduating from Colgate University, he worked at Plain and Fancy. Dave Bernier was an alumnus of the Culinary Institute of America, and his influence pointed Chris in that direction.

In those days, Dave and Maria lived in a tiny two-room apartment attached to the store's kitchen with their baby daughter, Emma. A few years later, after Chris and I graduated from the Culinary Institute of America, we moved into that little apartment and stayed a year. I'll never forget the sound of the big mixer churning the day's dough at 3:30 a.m., when the bakers started their work.

continued

Like Plain and Fancy, Wallace Station is in an old building on a scenic roadside, with lots of outside tables. At Plain and Fancy, large wooden bakery cases were filled with Danish, brownies, cookies, bagels, and breads—all baked right there on the premises overnight. Everything was made from scratch, and Dave had a delicious sandwich menu. Sadly, Plain and Fancy burned down, and Dave and Maria left the food business. We like to think that we're carrying on some of their food traditions, just a few miles south.

Before we opened Wallace Station, we drove by the empty storefront many times, and each time, Chris would comment how much it reminded him of Plain and Fancy. One day, we stopped and called the real estate agent's number. Within an hour, we heard from Larry Taylor, owner of the building. Larry is a wonderful salesman, and soon thereafter we were persuaded to bring back the old country store. Larry and his lovely wife, Denise, have been our landlords for sixteen years and counting. Larry helped us find the original store counter in the barn out back, signs, the enamel scale, and other parts of the old store.

Wallace Station's name derives from its location: Wallace, Kentucky. Wallace Station Historic District is on the National Register of Historic Places—a surviving example of a small railroad community. The community was named after Caleb Wallace, an appellate court judge who settled in Woodford County on the banks of South Elkhorn Creek around 1785 and owned a large estate on Old Frankfort Pike, near the Wallace area. Judge Wallace was known as a fierce advocate for religious freedom and public education. Through his lifelong friend James Madison, Wallace's writings likely influenced fellow Virginia colony resident Thomas Jefferson. Wallace helped found several colleges and universities, including Transylvania University in Lexington, and he was involved in establishing the public education system in Kentucky.

continued

The current building was built at the turn of the twentieth century by the McKinivan family. The McKinivans lived upstairs (now office space) and operated a store downstairs. The store sold feed, gasoline, machinery, fencing, and other farming necessities, as well as consumer goods such as fabric and groceries. At one time, the building also served as a post office.

An old rail bed along the tree line in the parking lot still marks the spot where trains used to run from Midway and surrounding towns to the phosphate mine just behind Wallace Station. The railroad lines were dismantled in 1941, and various owners continued to operate Wallace Station as a country store and grocery.

Panini comes from the Italian word *panino*, meaning "little sandwich." The American panini is usually made on a sturdy bread like focaccia or ciabatta filled with layers of ingredients, pressed, and lightly grilled (the bread recipes in chapter 2 work as well). Grilling in butter can produce a burned crust, especially when a longer cooking time is needed to heat a fully stuffed sandwich. We like to use butter oil—equal parts melted butter and canola oil—for grilling; the butter contributes great flavor, and the oil raises the smoke point.

Although panini presses are readily available for the home kitchen, these sandwiches can be duplicated at home without special equipment. Waffle irons make good pressed sandwiches, and many of them have interchangeable plates designed for sandwich making. A cast-iron skillet also makes a lovely panini, and you can use another heavy skillet or pan to press the sandwich.

Mulberry Meets Midway

Mulberry Meets Midway was on the first Wallace Station menu. Mulberry Street is the main drag through Little Italy in New York City. With all the wonderful tomatoes in season in July, we wanted to offer a caprese salad—fresh Mozzarella, heirloom tomatoes, and pesto—on a sandwich. This sandwich is best when the tomatoes and basil come right out of the garden.

4 ciabatta rolls or Italian rolls

½ cup Ethan's Pesto (recipe follows)

8 ounces fresh Mozzarella cheese, sliced

8 slices fresh tomato

½ cup roasted red peppers, julienned

2 tablespoons Mary's Italian Vinaigrette (see index)

4 handfuls baby greens

For each sandwich: Split a roll and toast lightly or grill. Spread pesto on each half. Cover one half with 2 ounces Mozzarella cheese, 2 tomato slices, 2 tablespoons roasted red peppers, a drizzle of Italian vinaigrette, and a handful of baby greens. Top with the other half roll and serve immediately.

Repeat with remaining ingredients.

Serves 4.

Ethan's Pesto

¼ cup toasted slivered almonds

2 large cloves garlic

4 ounces fresh basil, washed and stemmed (or 4 cups loosely packed basil leaves)

⅓ cup extra-virgin olive oil

¼ cup Parmesan cheese

½ teaspoon kosher salt

¼ teaspoon freshly ground black pepper

Pulverize almonds in a food processor and set aside.

Puree garlic in a food processor; add half the basil and pulse while drizzling in a couple tablespoons of oil. Add pulverized almonds, Parmesan, and the rest of the basil. Let the processor run a bit, then add the rest of the oil. Season with kosher salt and pepper.

Taste the pesto and check its consistency. It should be more like a sauce than a spread.

Makes ¾ cup.

Turkey Rachel

The Turkey Rachel, a variation of the well-known Reuben sandwich made with corned beef, has always been on the Wallace Station menu. This version is made with oven-roasted turkey, homemade Russian Dressing (as good on a salad as it is on a sandwich), and Creamy Coleslaw.

8 slices rye bread

1 cup Russian Dressing (recipe follows)

8 slices Swiss cheese

1 pound thinly sliced roasted turkey

1 cup Creamy Coleslaw (see index)

Butter oil for grilling (equal parts melted butter and canola oil)

For each sandwich: Warm sliced turkey in a grill pan or dry skillet. Lay out 2 slices of bread and cover both with Russian Dressing. Put 2 slices of Swiss cheese on 1 slice, then top with warm turkey. Spread ¼ cup coleslaw on the turkey and close the sandwich. Grill over medium heat in butter oil until golden brown and cheese has melted. Serve warm.

Repeat with remaining ingredients.

Serves 4.

Russian Dressing

1½ cups mayonnaise

½ cup ketchup

1½ tablespoons horseradish

1 teaspoon Worcestershire sauce

1½ teaspoons finely minced onion

¼ cup sweet pickle relish

Dash kosher salt

⅛ teaspoon freshly ground black pepper

Place all ingredients in a large bowl and blend thoroughly using a whisk and rubber spatula. Taste for seasoning. Chill at least 1 hour before using.

Makes 2½ cups.

Wallace Cubano

Our good friend Marta Miranda, a native of Cuba, inspired Wallace Station's Kentucky-style Cubano sandwich, made with Kentucky pulled pork, Kentucky ham, and Kentucky pickles.

---

8 slices white bread

1 cup Dijonnaise (recipe follows)

32 slices Pops' Habagardil pickles or other dill or sweet pickle slices

8 slices Swiss cheese

4 slices city ham

1¼ pounds Wallace Station Pulled Cubano Pork (see index)

Garlic Annatto Butter for warming and grilling (recipe follows)

For each sandwich: Warm 1 slice city ham and 5 ounces Pulled Cubano Pork in Garlic Annatto Butter in a small pan. Lay out 2 slices of bread. Spread 2 tablespoons Dijonnaise on both slices. Cover 1 slice of bread with 8 pickle slices and both slices with 1 slice Swiss cheese. To one side, add warm ham and then warm pork. Close the sandwich. Grill over medium heat in Garlic Annatto Butter until golden brown and cheese has melted. Serve warm.

Repeat with remaining ingredients.

Serves 4.

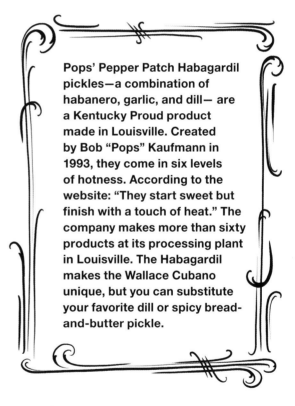

Pops' Pepper Patch Habagardil pickles—a combination of habanero, garlic, and dill— are a Kentucky Proud product made in Louisville. Created by Bob "Pops" Kaufmann in 1993, they come in six levels of hotness. According to the website: "They start sweet but finish with a touch of heat." The company makes more than sixty products at its processing plant in Louisville. The Habagardil makes the Wallace Cubano unique, but you can substitute your favorite dill or spicy bread-and-butter pickle.

Garlic Annatto Butter

Annatto seeds can be found in the Hispanic foods section of most grocery stores. The small, red, pebbly seeds come from a tropical fruit and impart a slightly spicy, earthy taste to this butter, as well as a deep yellow color.

4 ounces unsalted butter

¼ teaspoon annatto seeds

1½ teaspoons minced garlic

Melt butter in a small, heavy saucepan over medium-low heat. Add annatto and simmer 2 minutes. Add garlic and simmer about 30 seconds, until very aromatic. Remove from heat.

Cool to room temperature; then strain. Refrigerate until thickened and spreadable.

Dijonnaise

1 cup mayonnaise

¼ cup Dijon mustard

1½ teaspoons hot sauce

Dash kosher salt

Place all ingredients in a small bowl and whisk thoroughly until well combined. Taste for seasoning. Chill at least 30 minutes before serving to allow flavors to blend.

Makes 1¼ cups.

Bourbon Banh Mi

The Bourbon Banh Mi was created by Paul Hieb for Glenn's Creek Café at Woodford Reserve Distillery. Paul wanted to draw on the history of the area as well as the flavor of bourbon when he created this Kentucky version of banh mi. The crunch comes from local vegetables pickled in a sweet Asian brine spiced with sambal oelek, a chile paste flavored with garlic, ginger, and vinegar. The recipe originated at Holly Hill Inn, using bourbon in place of the traditional cognac and local jowl bacon (cured and smoked pork cheeks) in place of salt pork. At Woodford Reserve, Paul ordered a custom-ground pork and jowl bacon mixture from Stone Cross Farm to use as the base for his Country Pâté. The pâté can also be served on a cold lunch plate with pickled vegetables, salad, and crackers or crostini.

4 (6-inch) French baguettes

½ cup Bourbon Mayonnaise (see index)

12 ounces thinly sliced Chile-Ginger Roasted Pork (see index)

4 slices Country Pâté (recipe follows)

2 cups Asian Pickled Vegetables (recipe follows)

Fresh mint and cilantro leaves for garnish

For each sandwich: Split a baguette two-thirds of the way through, leaving a hinge, and warm briefly in a 300-degree F oven. Spread 1 tablespoon Bourbon Mayonnaise on each side of the split baguette, pile 3 ounces of pork on the bottom, tuck a slice of pâté on one side, and top with pickled vegetables. Garnish with fresh mint and cilantro.

Repeat with remaining ingredients.

Serves 4.

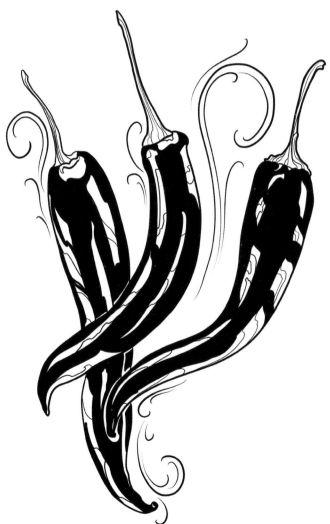

Country Pâté

2¼ pounds boneless pork shoulder butt, cut into 1-inch pieces

4 ounces bacon or jowl bacon

¼ cup finely chopped yellow onion

½ cup coarsely chopped parsley

1½ tablespoons minced garlic

1 tablespoon kosher salt

1 teaspoon freshly ground black pepper

1 teaspoon Pâté Spice (recipe follows)

2 tablespoons all-purpose flour

1 large egg

½ cup bourbon

½ cup heavy cream

Preheat oven to 300 degrees F.

Pulse pork and bacon in a food processor until nearly smooth but with some texture remaining. You will have to do this in batches. Freezing the meat for 10 minutes prior to grinding makes it easier to handle. Add onion, parsley, garlic, salt, pepper, and Pâté Spice and mix well. Refrigerate.

In a small bowl, combine flour, egg, bourbon, and cream and stir to blend—this is the *panade*. Add the panade to the ground meat and mix with a wooden spoon or your hands until the panade is incorporated and the forcemeat becomes sticky, about 1 minute. To test for seasoning, form the mixture into a small patty and fry in a small skillet. Taste and add seasoning as needed. The pâté will be served cold, so it will probably need a little extra salt.

Line an 8½-by-4½-by-2-inch loaf pan with plastic wrap, leaving enough overhang on the two long sides to fold over the top when filled (moistening the loaf pan first helps the plastic adhere). Fill the loaf pan with the pâté mixture, packing it to remove air pockets. Fold the plastic wrap over the top, and cover with foil.

Place the loaf pan in a high-sided roasting pan and add enough hot water to come halfway up the sides of the loaf pan. Bake until the interior of the pâté reaches 160 degrees F, about 2 hours. Because it was baked at a low temperature, the pâté might not look done, so it is important to check the internal temperature with a thermometer.

Carefully remove the roasting pan from the oven, remove the loaf pan from the water bath, and pour off excess fat. Cover the top with fresh plastic wrap. Set a 2-pound weight on top, and let the pâté cool to room temperature. Refrigerate until completely chilled —at least overnight and up to 1 week—before serving. Slice thinly for sandwiches or cold luncheon plates.

Makes 1 loaf.

Pâté Spice

This is my version of *Quatre-Epices*, the French spice mixture used for sausages, forcemeats, and terrines like the Country Pâté above. Use leftover spice mix in a marinade for roasted lamb, chicken, or pork.

1 teaspoon ground cloves

1 teaspoon ground nutmeg

1 teaspoon ground ginger

1 teaspoon ground coriander

2 teaspoons ground cinnamon

1 tablespoon white pepper

Combine all ingredients.

Asian Pickled Vegetables

PICKLING VINEGAR

¼ cup granulated sugar

½ cup unseasoned rice vinegar

1 teaspoon kosher salt

½ cup water

1 tablespoon chopped cilantro

½ teaspoon sambal oelek chile paste

VEGETABLES

1 cup peeled carrots, julienned

1 cup peeled daikon, julienned

1 cup red onion, thinly sliced into half moons

1 cup English cucumbers, thinly sliced into half moons

Heat sugar, vinegar, and salt in a glass measuring cup in the microwave until sugar has dissolved, about 1 minute. Cool to room temperature, then combine with the rest of the pickling ingredients and pour over prepared vegetables in a large bowl. Marinate at room temperature at least 30 minutes before using, stirring occasionally. This can be made ahead and refrigerated overnight.

Makes 1 quart.

East Hampton Hot Ham and Brie

The East Hampton Hot Ham and Brie was one of Chris's favorite sandwiches on the Plain and Fancy menu. The lunchtime line often extended out the deli's door, and I can still see Chris sweating over the little stove in the back kitchen, where it was hotter than blue blazes, griddling rosemary bread slices piled high with sliced ham, Brie, butter, and apple chutney.

In addition to nostalgia, we had a practical reason for adding this sandwich to the Wallace Station menu: we needed a city ham sandwich because not everyone likes country ham.

8 slices rye bread

½ cup Honey Mustard (recipe follows)

6 ounces thinly sliced Brie

24 thin slices Granny Smith apple

1 pound thinly sliced city ham

Butter oil for grilling (equal parts melted butter and canola oil)

For each sandwich: Warm 4 ounces of ham in a grill pan or dry skillet. Lay out 2 slices of bread and cover both with Honey Mustard. Place 4 Brie slices and 6 apple slices on one side, then cover with warm ham. Close the sandwich and grill in butter oil over medium heat until golden brown and cheese has melted. Serve warm.

Repeat with remaining ingredients.

Serves 4.

Honey Mustard

1 cup mayonnaise

¼ cup Dijon mustard

¼ cup honey

Place all ingredients in a small bowl and whisk thoroughly until well combined. Taste for seasoning. Chill at least 30 minutes before serving to allow flavors to blend.

Makes 1½ cups.

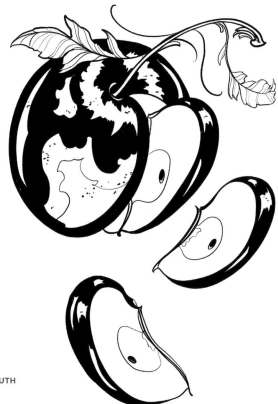

Merv's Ham and Jalapeño Panini

When my daughter, Willa, was a little girl, Merv Leckbee—our first customer at Wallace Station—gave her the most beautiful little horse on wheels and a blue sweater with a horse on the front. We had so much fun pulling the little horse around the room together, and it still stands on a shelf in Willa's room.

Merv wasn't only a kind and generous man—he was also the inspiration for the eponymous Merv's Ham and Jalapeño. Merv ate at Wallace Station at least three times a week and often ordered this custom-made sandwich, which wasn't on the menu. He also loved our Whitesburg Soup Beans (see chapter 6) and Blueberry Muffins (see chapter 1). After he passed away in 2006, we added the sandwich to the menu and named it after Merv as a remembrance.

8 slices bread (whole wheat, white, or rye)

1 cup Chipotle Mayonnaise
(see later in this chapter)

1 cup caramelized onions (see note below)

8 slices Provolone cheese

½ cup (about 8 slices per sandwich) Pickled Jalapeño Peppers, drained (recipe follows)

1 pound sliced city ham

Butter oil for grilling (equal parts melted butter and canola oil)

Note: To caramelize onions, start with more onions than you need, because they soften and shrink considerably as they cook. Sauté 2 large sliced sweet onions in canola oil or butter over medium heat, stirring often. Season lightly with salt. After about 10 minutes, the onions should begin to develop some color. Increase the heat to medium-high and continue to cook at least 10 minutes, stirring often. The onions should be golden brown in 20–25 minutes. If they start to stick, add a little water or white wine to deglaze the pan.

For each sandwich: Warm ham in a grill pan or dry skillet. Lay out 2 slices of bread. Spread 2 tablespoons Chipotle Mayonnaise on both slices, then cover 1 slice with ¼ cup caramelized onions, 8 jalapeño slices, and 2 slices Provolone. Top with warmed ham and close the sandwich. Grill in butter oil until golden brown and cheese has melted. Serve warm.

Repeat with remaining ingredients.

Serves 4.

Variation: Merv's Ham and Jalapeño can also be made as a quesadilla on a large flour tortilla with Horseradish Sauce (recipe follows) for dipping. Just layer the ingredients on the tortilla, fold it over, and grill in butter oil until golden brown on both sides.

Pickled Jalapeño Peppers

8 large jalapeños

1 garlic clove, halved

¾ cup white distilled vinegar

¾ cup water

3 tablespoons sugar

1½ tablespoons kosher or pickling salt

Wash and stem jalapeños. Thinly slice (with seeds) and set aside in a medium bowl.

Heat remaining ingredients in a small saucepan over medium-high heat. Bring to a boil and simmer until salt and sugar melt. Pour mixture over sliced jalapeños, immersing peppers in liquid. Cool to room temperature; then refrigerate.

Makes about 2 cups.

Horseradish Sauce

½ cup sour cream

1½ teaspoons finely minced onion

1½ teaspoons Worcestershire sauce

2 tablespoons prepared horseradish

½ teaspoon kosher salt

Pinch freshly ground black pepper

Place all ingredients in a medium bowl and blend thoroughly. Taste for seasoning. Chill at least 30 minutes before using.

Makes about ⅔ cup.

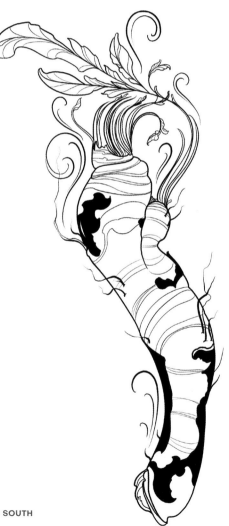

Inside Out Hot Brown

This sandwich is a variation of the hot Brown created in 1923 by chef Fred Schmidt at the Brown Hotel in Louisville, where it was served as a late-night supper. The hot Brown has become an iconic Kentucky dish, with every chef tweaking the recipe to suit his or her taste. The original hot Brown is open faced and must be eaten with a knife and fork, but this version can be eaten in hand as a sandwich.

Wallace Station opened with this sandwich, and its recipe is based on the popular hot Brown served at its sister fine-dining restaurant, the Holly Hill Inn in Midway.

8 slices white bread

1 cup White Cheddar Mornay Sauce (recipe follows)

8 tomato slices

1 pound thinly sliced roasted turkey

8 ounces thinly sliced city ham

12 slices bacon, cooked until crisp

Butter oil for grilling (equal parts melted butter and canola oil)

For each sandwich: Warm turkey, city ham, and bacon in a grill pan or dry skillet. Lay out 2 slices of bread. Cover both slices with 2 tablespoons White Cheddar Mornay Sauce, then cover one with 2 slices of tomato and one-quarter of the warmed meats. Close the sandwich. Grill in butter oil over medium heat until golden brown on both sides. Serve warm.

Repeat with remaining ingredients.

Serves 4.

White Cheddar Mornay Sauce

3 ounces unsalted butter

½ cup all-purpose flour

2 cups whole milk, slightly warm

1 cup shredded white Cheddar cheese

1 teaspoon kosher salt

Cayenne pepper to taste

In a heavy-bottomed saucepan, melt butter over medium heat, then whisk in flour until smooth. Cook 2 minutes, stirring periodically. Whisk in milk, stirring constantly to make sure ingredients are well mixed. Reduce heat to medium-low and bring to a simmer, stirring often, until mixture begins to thicken and bubble. Stir in shredded cheese, salt, and cayenne pepper. Remove from heat and continue to whisk until smooth.

Makes about 2½ cups.

Mediterranean Wrap

The elements of this wrap can be used as toppings for a hamburger. The Wallace Station Mediterranean Burger is dressed with Mediterranean Dip, Olive Salad, sliced tomatoes, lettuce, and red onion. Mediterranean Dip is also great with grilled vegetables or crudités or as a sauce for grilled lamb, beef, or chicken.

4 (10-inch) spinach tortillas

1 cup Mediterranean Dip (recipe follows)

4 handfuls baby greens

4 handfuls sprouts

1 (8-ounce) jar roasted red peppers, seeds removed, julienned

4 thin slices red onion

1 cup Olive Salad (recipe follows)

8 tomato slices

½ cup Mary's Italian Vinaigrette (see index)

For each wrap: Warm a spinach tortilla in a dry skillet or in the microwave until pliable. Spread ¼ cup Mediterranean Dip across the center of the tortilla, then top with a handful of baby greens, a handful of sprouts, ¼ cup roasted red peppers, a slice of red onion, ¼ cup Olive Salad, and 2 tomato slices. Drizzle with 2 tablespoons Italian vinaigrette. Fold the bottom half of the tortilla over the filling and pull to tighten. Fold in sides and roll tightly, then slice in half.

Repeat with remaining ingredients.

Serves 4.

Mediterranean Dip

1 cup mayonnaise

8 ounces Feta cheese, well drained and crumbled

1 cup pepperoncinis, well drained

½ cup sour cream

2 cloves garlic, minced

¼ cup capers, drained

½ teaspoon oregano

½ teaspoon freshly ground black pepper

1 tablespoon hot sauce

2 tablespoons minced fresh parsley

Place mayonnaise and Feta in a large bowl and blend well. Destem and chop pepperoncinis; if necessary, drain again after chopping to make sure pepperoncinis are almost dry. Add pepperoncinis and remaining ingredients to the bowl and combine. Taste for seasoning and chill before using.

Makes about 3 cups.

Olive Salad

Wallace Station first used this Olive Salad, from a recipe by Marie Ward of Lexington, on a muffuletta, which was on the original menu.

1 cup pepperoncinis, destemmed

½ cup (4 ounces) kalamata olives, pitted

¾ cup sliced Spanish olives

2 ounces (about ¼ cup)
canned diced pimientos

2 tablespoons capers

1¼ cups cauliflower florets

2 tablespoons finely chopped celery

2 tablespoons finely chopped red onion

¼ cup grated carrots

2 tablespoons Mary's Italian
Vinaigrette (see index)

Drain pepperoncinis and both types of olives and rough-chop. Place in a large bowl. Drain pimientos and capers and add to bowl.

Bring water to a boil in a small saucepan, add cauliflower florets, and cook until tender-crisp, about 3 minutes. Drain well, rinse with cold water, and cool. Roughly chop blanched cauliflower and add to bowl. Add celery, red onion, carrots, and vinaigrette. Fold together and mix well. Chill at least 1 hour before using so flavors can blend.

Makes 1 quart.

Santa Anita Club

Because Wallace Station sits in the middle of Thoroughbred horse country, sandwiches are often named for places of importance to the racing industry. Santa Anita Park in Arcadia, California, is the site of the annual Santa Anita Derby, one of the last prep races before the Kentucky Derby. This sandwich borrows ingredients and flavors from California to create a spicy rendition of the classic club sandwich.

8 slices bread (whole wheat, white, or rye)

½ cup Chipotle Mayonnaise (recipe follows)

½ cup Ethan's Guacamole (recipe follows)

1 pound thinly sliced oven-roasted turkey

8 slices Pepper Jack cheese

8 slices bacon, cooked until crisp

8 slices tomato

4 pieces leaf lettuce

For each sandwich: Toast 2 slices of bread. Spread 1 slice with 2 tablespoons Chipotle Mayonnaise and the other with 2 tablespoons Ethan's Guacamole. Cover the Chipotle Mayonnaise with 4 ounces of turkey, 2 slices Pepper Jack cheese, 2 strips bacon, 2 slices tomato, and 1 piece leaf lettuce. Top with the second slice of bread, cut, and serve immediately.

Repeat with remaining ingredients.

Serves 4.

Chipotle Mayonnaise

1 cup mayonnaise

1 tablespoon canned chipotle in adobo, finely minced (or more to taste)

In a small bowl, blend ingredients thoroughly using a whisk and rubber spatula.

Taste for seasoning. Add more chipotle to make the spread spicier. Chill well before using so flavors can blend.

Makes 1 cup.

Ethan's Guacamole

2 cloves garlic

½ jalapeño pepper, seeds and ribs removed

4 avocados, peeled and seeded

Juice of 2 limes (about 2½ tablespoons)

1 tablespoon minced cilantro

½ teaspoon cumin

1 teaspoon kosher salt

Mince garlic and jalapeño pepper together and put in a medium bowl. Add avocados and mash with a fork. Add remaining ingredients and mix well. Taste for salt and seasonings and chill 30 minutes so flavors can blend. Placing an avocado seed in the center of the guacamole helps keep it from browning.

Makes 2½ cups.

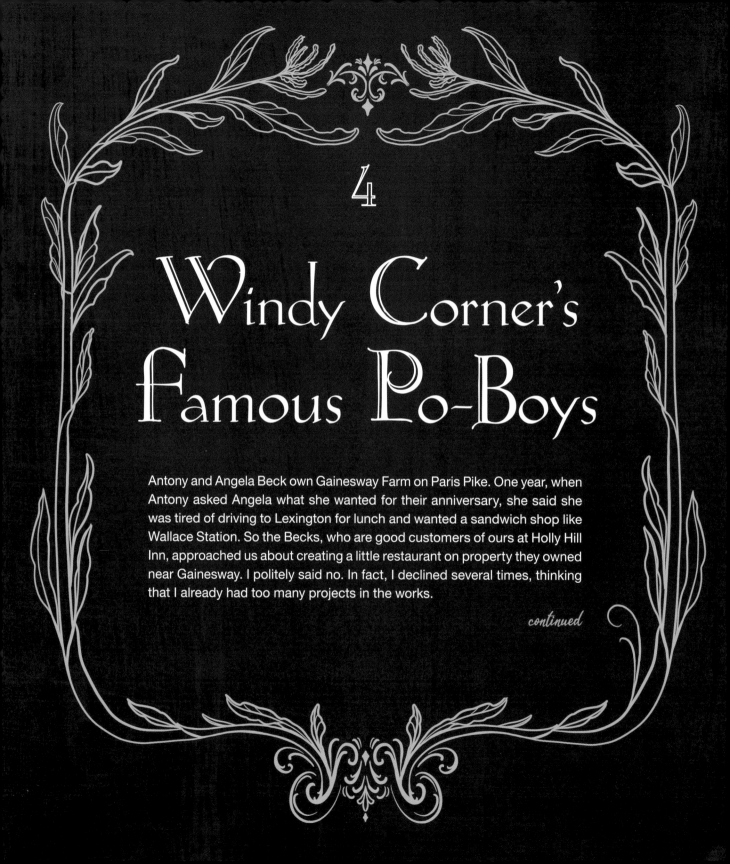

4

Windy Corner's Famous Po-Boys

Antony and Angela Beck own Gainesway Farm on Paris Pike. One year, when Antony asked Angela what she wanted for their anniversary, she said she was tired of driving to Lexington for lunch and wanted a sandwich shop like Wallace Station. So the Becks, who are good customers of ours at Holly Hill Inn, approached us about creating a little restaurant on property they owned near Gainesway. I politely said no. In fact, I declined several times, thinking that I already had too many projects in the works.

continued

Thankfully, Mr. Beck persisted and asked for our advice about what could be done with that corner property at the junction of Muir Station and Bryan Station Roads, just a few miles from the Bourbon County line. The existing structure was a rundown cinder-block building that had once housed a country store and was now moldy and rotted, stained with cigarette smoke, littered with old beer bottles, and sat atop leaking underground gasoline tanks. But that day, we created a vision of a place that would welcome local folks with local food, local goods, and live music. Joan Gaines (previous owner of Gainesway Farm, along with her husband, John) told me that her son, Thomas, would often run down to that corner store for baloney sandwiches and other treats. Back then, the name of the store was Windy Corner, and we opened our own Windy Corner Market and Restaurant in 2010.

We were thrilled to bring the store back to life with its original name. Our building plan was based on the style of a country store in Troy, Kentucky, in Woodford County, that has since become a residence. People think the building has always been there, but Mr. Beck built it from the ground up in 2009 after demolishing the original building. Like the gardens at Gainesway, we perfume our lot with lavender; we have fig trees growing out back and a wonderful lawn all around. Silks from neighboring horse farms line the walls, along with shelves of Kentucky honey, sorghum, grits, bourbon balls, and so much more. Windy Corner has become a popular destination for both locals and tourists and has received national media attention.

continued

So why Po-Boys? In December 2009, Chris and I traveled to New Orleans with the VisitLex team to prepare a bourbon dinner at Dickie Brennan's famous restaurant, Bourbon House, in honor of his induction as a Kentucky Colonel. Mr. Brennan was the soul of hospitality, taking us on a tour of his beautiful restaurants and spending an afternoon with us, telling us about his family, the aftereffects of Hurricane Katrina, and his passion for Po-Boy sandwiches. It was Mr. Brennan's dream to establish a Po-Boy trail to support and celebrate the mom-and-pop shops that were still struggling to recover from Katrina.

At the time, we were trying to develop a concept for the menu at Windy Corner Market, and as we toured New Orleans, we realized that the humble Po-Boy sandwich was a great vehicle for Kentucky-raised pork, chicken, country ham, beef, and catfish.

Windy Corner imports its traditional French-style loaf from Gambino's bakery in New Orleans. I like this loaf because it has a very thin, crispy crust and a soft interior, so it encases the filling without dominating its flavors. Gambino's has been baking these great loaves for almost 100 years down in New Orleans. I was thrilled to be able to get the bread in Kentucky.

Windy Corner Market uses the traditional Po-Boy setup: shredded lettuce, tomato, and pickle (referred to as LTP) and a special sauce created by chef Sara Gibbs. Every Po-Boy shop has its own version of a Po-Boy sauce. We also make a tasty remoulade that is delicious with seafood. Like every great sandwich, the Po-Boy has a million variations, and our customers order them however they like. We also serve Po-Boys at Zim's Café, the restaurant we opened in 2018 in the renovated historic Fayette County courthouse in downtown Lexington.

Windy Corner Fish and Seafood Po-Boys

My parents lived in New Orleans for a time, where they came to love an oyster Po-Boy. My dad, Ray, declared the one at Windy Corner the best he has ever had. Windy Corner's shrimp and catfish Po-Boys are popular, too.

1 pound fish or seafood of your choice (crawfish, catfish, oysters, or shrimp)

1 cup Weisenberger Mill Fish Batter Mix or Tyler's Cornmeal Dredge (see index)

Canola oil for frying

4 (6-inch) Po-Boy baguettes or French baguettes

½ cup Special Sauce (recipe follows)

2 cups (about 6 ounces) shredded iceberg lettuce

8 thin tomato slices

12 Pops' Habagardil or other dill pickle slices

¾ cup Lisa's Remoulade (recipe follows)

For the seafood: Heat canola oil to 350 degrees F. Dredge fish or seafood in dry batter mix or cornmeal dredge, shake off excess breading, and fry until cooked through and golden brown. Drain well in a fry basket or on paper towels. Use immediately.

For each sandwich: Split a baguette partway through, leaving a hinge. Open the bread and slather 2 tablespoons Special Sauce on the bottom. Add one-quarter of the warm fish or seafood, then cover with ½ cup lettuce, 2 tomato slices, 3 pickle slices, and a dollop of Lisa's Remoulade. Serve immediately.

Repeat with remaining ingredients.

Serves 4.

All our restaurants serve US Department of Agriculture (USDA)–inspected Kentucky Proud channel catfish and blue catfish from Lake Barkley and Kentucky Lake in the western part of the state. Lake Barkley has a large population of smaller catfish, while Kentucky Lake, which is deeper and colder, grows bigger catfish. Lake conditions determine where our fish come from. Eating the bottom-feeders (which catfish are) in lakes helps other fish populations thrive. Heath Frailley from F&F Fish Market in Calhoun, Kentucky, catches and processes all our catfish. If F&F runs short, we buy farm-raised catfish from certified US catfish farmers.

Most catfish consumed in the United States is imported from either Vietnam or China. Vietnamese catfish is a different species of fish altogether and is often called basa or swai. Back in the early days at Windy Corner, my young chef proudly told me about the great deal he got on Asian catfish. I went ballistic. It is not legal to call Vietnamese basa "catfish" in the United States. Fish coming from Vietnam and China can be contaminated with carcinogens, banned antibiotics, and salmonella.

American catfish are sustainably farmed and highly regulated by the USDA and endorsed by the National Audubon Society and Monterey Bay Aquarium as a safe and sustainable choice. Plus, because these catfish are raised in freshwater and fed a vegetarian diet, they are very low in contaminants such as mercury.

We have so much beautiful freshwater in Kentucky, and catfish have been part of our fishing culture for hundreds of years. You can't beat a fresh Kentucky catfish rolled in Weisenberger Mill breading—delicious!

Special Sauce

Our Po-Boy sauce is a beautiful pale green and has a tangy herbal punch.

---

1 cup mayonnaise

2 tablespoons Dijon mustard

¼ teaspoon kosher salt

¼ teaspoon dry mustard

¼ teaspoon white pepper

¼ teaspoon freshly ground black pepper

½ bunch curly parsley, stems removed

2 green onions, thinly sliced

1 clove garlic, chopped

1½ tablespoons canola oil

Place mayonnaise, Dijon mustard, salt, dry mustard, and white and black pepper in a medium bowl. Set aside.

Add parsley, green onions, garlic, and oil to a food processor. Puree until smooth. Add this to the mayonnaise and spice mixture and blend well.

Chill 30 minutes before using.

Makes about 1½ cups.

Spicy Special Sauce

For an extra lick of heat, use this spicy version on any Po-Boy. The Windy Corner Market kitchen staff prefers Crystal hot sauce from New Orleans, but any Louisiana-style hot sauce can be used.

---

1 cup mayonnaise

2 teaspoons grated sweet onion

1 teaspoon fresh lemon juice

½ teaspoon minced garlic

1 teaspoon Crystal hot sauce

¼ teaspoon cayenne pepper

¼ teaspoon white pepper

1 teaspoon ground sweet paprika

Blend all ingredients thoroughly in a medium bowl. Chill at least 30 minutes before serving.

Makes about 1 cup.

Lisa's Remoulade

1 cup mayonnaise

1 teaspoon whole-grain mustard

1 teaspoon dried tarragon

1 teaspoon ground sweet paprika

½ teaspoon cayenne pepper

1 tablespoon capers, drained and minced

1 tablespoon minced fresh parsley

1½ tablespoons fresh lemon juice

½ teaspoon minced garlic

In a large bowl, mix all ingredients thoroughly with a whisk. Chill at least 30 minutes before serving.

Makes about 1 cup.

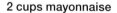

Tartar Sauce

Another option for a fish or seafood Po-Boy is our take on classic creamy tartar sauce. This recipe was inspired by sauce gribiche, a French sauce made with hard-boiled egg that is most often paired with fish, boiled chicken, or cold terrines.

2 cups mayonnaise

1½ teaspoons Dijon mustard

1 teaspoon fresh lemon juice

½ teaspoon kosher salt

¼ teaspoon cayenne pepper

2 tablespoons minced fresh parsley

¼ shallot, minced

2 tablespoons dill pickle slices, minced

1 hard-boiled egg, finely chopped

2 tablespoons capers, drained and chopped

Mix all ingredients in a large bowl. Chill at least 30 minutes before using.

Makes about 2½ cups.

Kentucky Combination Po-Boy

Traditionally, the Po-Boy crowd calls meat and cheese the "combination." To make the Kentucky Combination, Windy Corner uses country ham and Swiss cheese.

4 (6-inch) Po-Boy baguettes
or French baguettes

½ cup Special Sauce (see
earlier in this chapter)

2 cups (about 6 ounces)
shredded iceberg lettuce

8 thin tomato slices

12 dill pickle slices

1 pound thinly sliced country ham

8 slices Swiss cheese

For each sandwich: Split a baguette partway through, leaving a hinge. Open the bread and slather 2 tablespoons Special Sauce on the bottom. Cover with ½ cup shredded lettuce, 2 tomato slices, 3 pickle slices, 4 ounces country ham, and 2 slices Swiss cheese.

Repeat with remaining ingredients.

Serves 4.

Kentucky Boy

In Louisiana, classic Po-Boys are often made with slow-cooked pot roast, and the bread is soaked with "debris" gravy. To create one that expressed Kentucky, pulled pork was the obvious choice because Kentuckians love pulled pork. We soak the bread in Bourbon Barbecue Sauce instead of debris gravy and top it with our own bourbon-spiked beer cheese. For an extra twist, we fry the pickles.

4 (6-inch) Po-Boy baguettes
or French baguettes

½ cup Special Sauce (see
earlier in this chapter)

24–28 thinly sliced red onion rings

2 cups (about 6 ounces)
shredded iceberg lettuce

1¼ pound Wallace Station Pulled
Cubano Pork (see index)

½ cup Kentucky River Beer
Cheese (recipe follows)

½ cup Bourbon Barbecue Sauce
(see later in this chapter)

24 Fried Pickle slices (recipe follows)

For each sandwich: Split a baguette partway through, leaving a hinge. Open the bread and slather 2 tablespoons Special Sauce on the bottom. Cover with 6–7 onion rings, ½ cup shredded lettuce, 5 ounces pulled pork, 2 tablespoons warm beer cheese, 2 tablespoons barbecue sauce, and 6 warm pickle slices. Using a squeeze bottle helps distribute the barbecue sauce evenly over the sandwich ingredients.

Repeat with remaining ingredients.

Serves 4.

Fried Pickles

24 dill pickle slices

½ cup Weisenberger Mill Fish Batter Mix
or Tyler's Cornmeal Dredge (see index)

Canola oil for frying

Heat canola oil in a deep skillet or small kettle fryer to 350 degrees F. Drain pickle slices slightly and dredge in dry batter mix or cornmeal dredge. Lower carefully into hot oil and fry 4 minutes or until golden brown. Drain well. Use to garnish sandwiches, or serve as a snack with remoulade for dipping.

Kentucky River Beer Cheese

Beer cheese has become a culinary icon of central Kentucky, especially around the Kentucky River and in Winchester, home of the Beer Cheese Festival. There are copious recipes and fierce competition about which one is best. I have never met a beer cheese I didn't like, but my favorite is this recipe, inspired by longtime Lexington grocer Walt Barbour. It's fantastic on sandwiches, especially burgers and Po-Boys.

Make this beer cheese right before using it on a Po-Boy because it's easier to spread at room temperature than when chilled. Leftover spread works as a traditional Kentucky party snack served with crackers or crisp fresh vegetables. This version is spicy, so if you want to tame the heat, cut down on the cayenne and hot sauce.

---

2 (6½-ounce) tubs spreadable Cheddar cheese

2 tablespoons Kentucky Bourbon Barrel Ale or your favorite beer

1 tablespoon Kentucky bourbon

2 teaspoons Crystal hot sauce

2 teaspoons Worcestershire sauce

½ teaspoon onion powder

½ teaspoon ground sweet paprika

½ teaspoon granulated garlic or ¼ teaspoon garlic powder

½ teaspoon white pepper

½ teaspoon cayenne pepper

Immerse tubs of Cheddar in a bowl of hot water until softened, or soften in a microwave 1 minute on 30 percent power. If the cheese is still firm, stir and continue to microwave on 30 percent power in 15-second increments until softened.

Whip cheese and Bourbon Barrel Ale in a mixer, then add remaining ingredients. Continue to whip until well blended. Taste for seasoning.

Chill until ready to use.

Makes about 2 cups.

Barbecue Boy

The inspiration for the Barbecue Boy came from Billy's Barbecue, owned by Bob Stubblefield, in the Chevy Chase neighborhood of Lexington. I first went to Billy's when I was a student at the University of Kentucky, and I loved the Deluxe Pulled Pork Sandwich. After thirty-seven years in business, Billy's closed in 2015, which was a big loss to the community.

4 (6-inch) Po-Boy baguettes or French baguettes

½ cup Special Sauce (see earlier in this chapter)

24–28 thinly sliced red onion rings

1 cup shredded white Cheddar cheese

1¼ pounds Wallace Station Pulled Cubano Pork (see index)

½ cup Bourbon Barbecue Sauce (recipe follows)

1 cup Creamy Coleslaw (see index)

12 Pops' Habagardil or other dill pickle slices

For each sandwich: Split a baguette partway through, leaving a hinge. Open the bread and slather 2 tablespoons Special Sauce on the bottom. Cover with 6–7 onion rings, ¼ cup shredded Cheddar, 5 ounces warm pulled pork, 2 tablespoons barbecue sauce, and ½ cup coleslaw. Top with 3 pickle slices.

Repeat with remaining ingredients.

Serves 4.

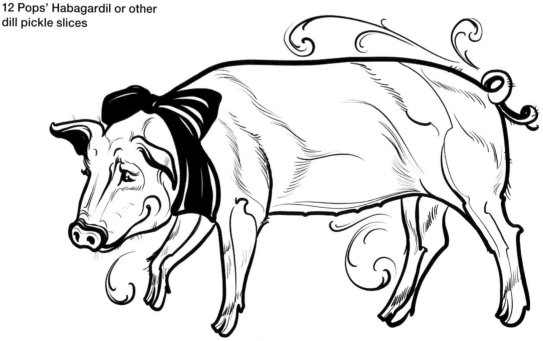

Bourbon Barbecue Sauce

This sauce marries the flavors of bourbon and cola in a slightly spicy, tangy barbecue sauce that works as well on tofu as it does on pork or chicken.

1 tablespoon unsalted butter

½ teaspoon minced garlic

1 cup ketchup

1 cup cola

3 tablespoons Worcestershire sauce

¼ cup steak sauce

¼ teaspoon cayenne pepper

¼ teaspoon freshly ground black pepper

½ teaspoon dry mustard

2 tablespoons white distilled vinegar

2 tablespoons bourbon

Melt butter in a 2-quart heavy-bottomed saucepan over medium heat. Add minced garlic and sauté 30 seconds. Whisk in remaining ingredients except bourbon and mix well.

Bring sauce to a boil, then reduce heat to medium-low and simmer 30 minutes. The sauce should be slightly thickened. Add bourbon and simmer another 10–15 minutes.

Serve warm on Po-Boys or other sandwiches. Refrigerate any leftovers.

Makes 2½ cups.

Smoked Roast Beef Po-Boy

Although this sandwich requires multiple steps, the result is well worth the effort. It was on the first Windy Corner menu and was inspired by the classic New Orleans "debris-style" roast beef Po-Boys. Here, chuck roast is smoked and then braised until fork tender and moistened with dark, rich Creole Gravy.

4 (6-inch) Po-Boy baguettes or French baguettes

½ cup Special Sauce (see earlier in this chapter)

1¼ pounds warm Windy Corner Pulled Beef (recipe follows)

Creole Gravy (recipe follows)

2 cups (about 6 ounces) shredded iceberg lettuce

8 thin tomato slices

12 Pops' Habagardil or other dill pickle slices

For each sandwich: Split a baguette partway through, leaving a hinge. Open the bread and slather 2 tablespoons Special Sauce on the bottom. Cover with pulled beef and several tablespoons of Creole Gravy. Garnish with ½ cup shredded lettuce and 2 tomato slices and top with 3 pickle slices.

Repeat with remaining ingredients.

Serves 4.

Creole Gravy

2 cups strained pan juices from Windy Corner Pulled Beef (recipe follows)

3 tablespoons roux (see note below)

1½ tablespoons Worcestershire sauce

Kosher salt and freshly ground black pepper to taste

Heat pan juices in a saucepan over medium-high heat until the liquid comes to a boil. Whisk in warm roux and cook until thickened. Add Worcestershire sauce, then season with salt and pepper to taste. Keep warm.

Makes 2 cups.

Note: To make a simple roux, melt 2 tablespoons unsalted butter in a small skillet over medium-low heat, stir in 2½ tablespoons all-purpose flour, and cook about 6 minutes, stirring constantly until the mixture has thickened and darkened in color to a light brown and has a nutty aroma. Cool slightly before adding to liquid.

Windy Corner Pulled Beef

2½-pound chuck roast

1 teaspoon kosher salt

½ teaspoon freshly ground black pepper

⅛ teaspoon garlic powder

1 teaspoon minced fresh thyme

1 (14½-ounce) can whole tomatoes

1 cup chopped onion

½ cup chopped carrot

½ cup chopped celery

Beef stock to cover

Mix kosher salt, black pepper, garlic powder, and thyme together and rub on all sides of the chuck roast.

Heat grill to medium-high. Sear chuck roast on both sides, then move it off the heat and cook indirectly at about 200 degrees F for 2 hours, using smoking chips. Keep the smoke going for the entire cooking time.

Remove the meat from the grill and place in a deep roasting pan. Crush whole tomatoes by hand and scatter over the beef, along with onion, carrot, celery, and enough beef stock to cover the meat halfway. Cover and roast in the oven at 325 degrees F until the internal temperature reaches 200 degrees F and the meat is fork tender, 2–2½ hours.

Remove the meat from the liquid and place on a cutting board. Remove visible bits of fat and discard. Shred the meat with two forks. Set aside. Separate and discard fat from the pan juices. Strain and reserve the warm pan juices for Creole Gravy.

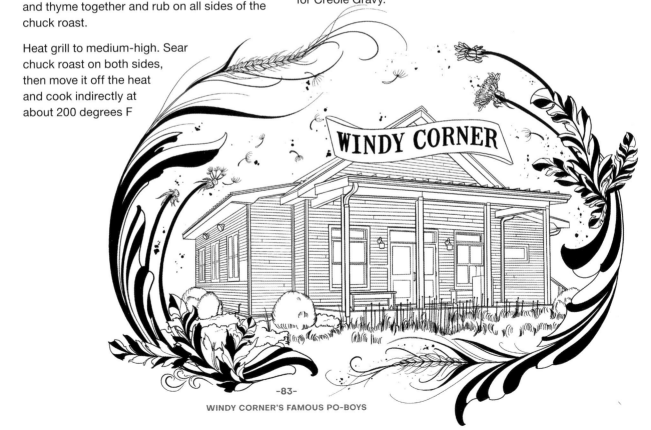

WINDY CORNER'S FAMOUS PO-BOYS

Tofu Boy for Topher

While at Colgate University, Chris's nickname was "Tofu" or "Topher." I love alliteration, and I also love fried tofu, so when Windy Corner's menu needed a vegetarian Po-Boy, that's where the name came from. Tofu's mild flavor makes it a great vehicle for sauces.

4 (6-inch) Po-Boy baguettes
or French baguettes

½ cup Special Sauce (see
earlier in this chapter)

2 cups (about 6 ounces)
shredded iceberg lettuce

8 thin tomato slices

12 Pops' Habagardil or other dill pickle slices

24–28 cubes Fried Tofu (recipe follows)

½ cup Bourbon Barbecue Sauce
(see earlier in this chapter)

1 cup Sassy Sorghum Slaw (see index)

For each sandwich: Split a baguette partway through, leaving a hinge. Open the bread and slather 2 tablespoons Special Sauce on the

bottom. Cover with ½ cup shredded lettuce, 2 tomato slices, 3 pickle slices, 6–7 cubes fried tofu, 2 tablespoons barbecue sauce, and ¼ cup sorghum slaw.

Repeat with remaining ingredients.

Serves 4.

Fried Tofu

10 ounces extra-firm fresh tofu,
drained and cut in ½-inch cubes

1 cup Weisenberger Mill Fish Batter Mix
or Tyler's Cornmeal Dredge (see index)

Canola oil for frying

Heat oil to 350 degrees F. Dredge tofu cubes in dry batter mix or cornmeal dredge and fry 4–5 minutes until crisp and golden on the outside. Drain well.

Buffalo Catfish Sandwich

Although not a Po-Boy, this spicy sandwich from our restaurant Smithtown Seafood is another interesting way to use Kentucky Proud catfish. Jonathan Sanning created the perfect condiment, Blue Cheese Celery Slaw, using elements of the classic accompaniments for buffalo-style chicken wings.

1 pound catfish fillets, cut into strips or fingers and soaked in beer 15 minutes

1 cup Weisenberger Mill Fish Batter Mix or Tyler's Cornmeal Dredge (see index)

Canola oil for frying

¼ cup Buffalo Sauce (recipe follows)

4 sourdough, brioche, or other sturdy buns

1 cup Blue Cheese Celery Slaw (recipe follows)

12 Pops' Habagardil or other dill pickle slices

For the catfish: Heat canola oil to 350 degrees F. Dredge fish in dry batter mix or cornmeal dredge, shake off excess breading, and fry until cooked through and golden brown. Drain well in a fry basket or on paper towels. Toss with Buffalo Sauce. Use immediately.

For each sandwich: Pile ¼ cup Blue Cheese Celery Slaw on the bottom of a bun. Add one-quarter of the catfish and cover with 3 pickle slices. Serve immediately.

Repeat with remaining ingredients.

Serves 4.

Buffalo Sauce

Be forewarned that this sauce is spicy. The addition of fresh jalapeño and three dried chile powders gives it an extra kick. Leftover sauce can be kept for a week and warmed before using.

4 tablespoons unsalted butter

½ jalapeño pepper, minced

1 garlic clove, minced

½ teaspoon ancho chile powder

⅛ teaspoon chipotle chile powder

Generous pinch cayenne

1 cup Crystal hot sauce

Melt butter in a sauté pan over medium heat. Add jalapeño, garlic, chile powders, and cayenne and sauté until jalapeño begins to soften, about 1 minute. Stir in hot sauce and remove from heat. Cool slightly before using.

Makes about 1 cup.

Blue Cheese Celery Slaw

This slaw is best on the day it is made but is perfectly acceptable on day two. Crisp green celery should be used because it adds the most crunch to the slaw.

2 cups shredded red cabbage

2 cups celery, thinly sliced on the bias

3 green onions, thinly sliced on the bias

⅓ cup blue cheese crumbles

½ cup Blue Cheese Vinaigrette (recipe follows)

Kosher salt and freshly ground black pepper to taste

Toss all ingredients together in a large bowl. Taste for seasoning. Chill at least 30 minutes before serving.

Makes about 3½ cups.

Blue Cheese Vinaigrette

A high-quality aged blue cheese works best for this dressing. The type of blue cheese determines how much salt you will need, because some are saltier than others. Leftover dressing is perfect on a crisp, cold wedge of iceberg lettuce garnished with diced tomato, red onion, and crumbled bacon.

1 cup (4 ounces) blue cheese crumbles

¼ cup sweet onion, chopped

2 tablespoons malt vinegar

1 tablespoon fresh lemon juice

⅛ teaspoon Crystal hot sauce

1½ teaspoons Worcestershire sauce

½ teaspoon freshly ground black pepper

½ cup canola oil

Kosher salt to taste

Place half the blue cheese crumbles in the bowl of a food processor, along with onion, vinegar, lemon juice, hot sauce, Worcestershire sauce, and black pepper. Process until well blended and smooth, then drizzle in canola oil. Stir in remaining blue cheese and taste for seasoning. Add kosher salt as needed.

Makes 1¼ cups.

5

Burgers

The local hamburger is a marker of success for me because it means that locally raised beef is affordable and accessible to a wide range of customers. Twenty years ago, getting locally raised meats to an inspected processor was difficult. People talked about local burgers, but most restaurants were not serving them as part of the regular menu. At Holly Hill Inn, the menu featured steaks, but we had no outlet for ground beef. At that time, Wallace Station's kitchen was too small to cook burgers because we were baking all our breads and cookies there. To help solve the glut of hamburger from one of my favorite farms, Elmwood Stock Farm in neighboring Scott County, we started the Hamburger Hootenanny. For several years, we hosted a huge Memorial Day picnic on the grounds of Holly Hill Inn. Hundreds of folks came to listen to music on the front lawn and munch on delicious Elmwood burgers.

continued

When we opened Windy Corner in 2010, we wanted to sell burgers made with locally raised beef. Launching Windy Corner with a big beautiful line of burgers was pure joy. At the time, "pink slime," a puree of beef trimmings added to hamburger patties to reduce shrinkage and fat content, was making headlines. This by-product of the giant factory burger mixing and shaping process sure wasn't appetizing. By contrast, Windy Corner's burgers were 100 percent fresh ground beef, with no fillers or additives, from cattle raised by Kentucky farm families.

Two years later, we opened the Midway School Bakery (now the Midway Bakery), freeing up Wallace Station's kitchen. A remodel allowed the Wallace Station staff to begin a great burger program there.

Companywide—at Wallace Station, Windy Corner Market, Honeywood, Zim's Café, and Smithtown Seafood (yes, our fish shop has great burgers!)—100,000 local hamburgers are sold annually, not to mention the ground beef used for chili and meatloaf. This commitment to locally raised beef helps farmers increase their efficiency and reduce food waste, encouraging consumption of the entire animal. Our restaurants use a few select producers—Stone Cross Farm in Taylorsville, Elmwood Stock Farm, Blackhawk Farms near Princeton, and others—to deliver great-tasting and nutritious burgers to customers. For burgers, I prefer an 80/20 grind (80 percent lean, 20 percent fat).

STONE CROSS FARM

Patrick and Leeta Kennedy of Stone Cross Farm in Taylorsville, Kentucky, have been my farming partners for more than a decade. Their pigs and beef cattle are raised without steroids, hormones, or antibiotics. Patrick was one of the first farmers to deliver his products to restaurants in Louisville and central Kentucky himself, solving a big problem for small farmers: distribution. As long as I've known Patrick, he has been a pragmatic problem solver. Stone Cross sausages, chops, and burgers are delicious. Every January for the past twelve years, I've purchased a pig for my church's Epiphany celebration. And each year, everyone swears it's the best one yet.

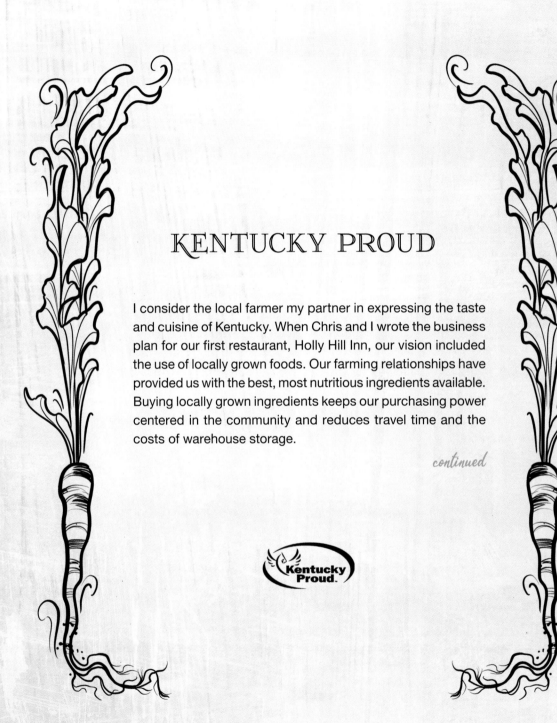

KENTUCKY PROUD

I consider the local farmer my partner in expressing the taste and cuisine of Kentucky. When Chris and I wrote the business plan for our first restaurant, Holly Hill Inn, our vision included the use of locally grown foods. Our farming relationships have provided us with the best, most nutritious ingredients available. Buying locally grown ingredients keeps our purchasing power centered in the community and reduces travel time and the costs of warehouse storage.

continued

"Kentucky Proud" is the official state marketing program for agricultural products. Products that are grown, produced, and processed by in-state farms and related farm businesses are allowed to use the Kentucky Proud trademarked logo to show consumers that they are from Kentucky. Since the program's inception in 2002, all our restaurants have been certified as Kentucky Proud. Kentucky Proud incentive money paid for Holly Hill Inn's first website and helped finance the mailing of its newsletter.

We also participate in the Buy Local program, designed to connect chefs and restaurants to local growers. We submit receipts to the state to verify purchases, and in return, we receive up to 15 percent of the cost of our purchases of farm-gate goods—that is, fresh ingredients that cross over the farm gate. These include all fruits, vegetables, eggs, meats, fish, milk, and farm-processed foods such as cheese, sorghum, honey, and nuts. The amount any restaurant can receive is capped at $12,000 per year, with a lifetime cap of $36,000. We earmarked this money for advertising our connection to Kentucky's agricultural community. All our restaurants, except for the most recent additions, have met their lifetime caps and graduated from the Buy Local program.

As our restaurant group has grown, the Kentucky Proud program has also grown into more than fifteen programs that target Appalachia-grown and -produced goods, US veteran farmers, Kentucky wine, farm-to-school programs, and others. Kentucky is a leader across the nation in branding its farm goods and connecting its farmers to new programs to help market their products. Our family of restaurants is closing in on $3 million in Kentucky Proud purchases since 2001, helping to fulfill one of my missions as a restaurateur: to increase farm income in Kentucky.

Big Brown Burger

In 2009, Guy Fieri and his *Diners, Drive-Ins and Dives* television crew visited Wallace Station to tape an episode that aired March 20, 2010, on the Food Network (it can still be seen in reruns). He tried the fried chicken and the Big Brown Burger, which he rated as "one of his top 5 burgers of all time." The Big Brown continues to be the most popular choice for first-timers at Wallace Station.

4 sturdy hamburger buns

4 (6-ounce) burger patties

Salt and pepper for seasoning

1 cup White Cheddar Mornay Sauce (see index)

4 slices city ham

8 slices bacon, cooked until crisp

8 tomato slices

Cook burgers on a grill or in a skillet to the desired temperature, seasoning with salt and pepper.

For each burger: While burgers are cooking, lay out a hamburger bun and cover both sides with 2 tablespoons Mornay sauce. Cover one side with 1 ham slice and the other side with 2 strips bacon. Warm both sides in a skillet, meat side down, until Mornay sauce melts. To the bottom half of the bun, add a burger and 2 tomato slices. Cover with the bun top and serve immediately.

Repeat with remaining ingredients.

Serves 4.

JUST A FEW MILES SOUTH

Mabel's Nut Burger

Sara Gibbs, coauthor of this book, first came to work with me in 2009 at the Woodford Reserve Distillery, where we were launching a lunch counter in the Visitor's Center for guests touring the facility. Sara wrote a masterful recipe book for the lunch counter, researched her ideas thoroughly, and built a wonderful menu. We made a good team, so when I began to think about the menu for the yet-to-be-built Windy Corner Market, I brought in Sara. She tested and wrote recipes, brainstormed ideas with me, and spent many hours costing ingredients and setting up inventory lists. I was looking for a creative signature burger for Windy Corner, and Sara told me about her mom, Mabel Thompson, and her famous nut burger.

Mabel grew up in the eastern panhandle of West Virginia. In the 1940s, she went to a diner in nearby Cumberland, Maryland, that served a burger with a peanut dressing. Mabel fell in love with the flavor combinations, and Sara grew up eating the re-created nut burger at her mother's table. It is my favorite burger at Windy Corner. We named the burger for Mabel, who passed away in 2015. I am grateful to her daughter, Sara, for the years of culinary dedication, inspiration, and true friendship.

---

4 sturdy hamburger buns

4 (6-ounce) burger patties

Salt and pepper for seasoning

½ cup Slightly Spicy Peanut Mayonnaise (recipe follows)

1 cup Creamy Coleslaw (see index)

Cook burgers on a grill or in a skillet to the desired temperature, seasoning with salt and pepper.

For each burger: While burgers are cooking, lay out a hamburger bun. Cover the underside of the top with 2–3 tablespoons peanut mayonnaise. Place a burger on the bottom half of the bun and top with ¼ cup coleslaw. Cover with the bun top and serve immediately.

Repeat with remaining ingredients.

Serves 4.

Slightly Spicy Peanut Mayonnaise

Dry-roasted peanuts are best for this spread because they provide the perfect amount of crunch.

1½ cups dry-roasted peanuts

Heaping ½ cup mayonnaise, enough to bind peanuts

½ teaspoon Sriracha hot sauce, or more to taste

Pulse peanuts in a food processor just until rough-chopped, leaving fairly large chunks. These larger pieces give the mayo more bite and texture. Pour peanuts into a small bowl and fold in mayonnaise and Sriracha to taste.

Makes about 1½ cups.

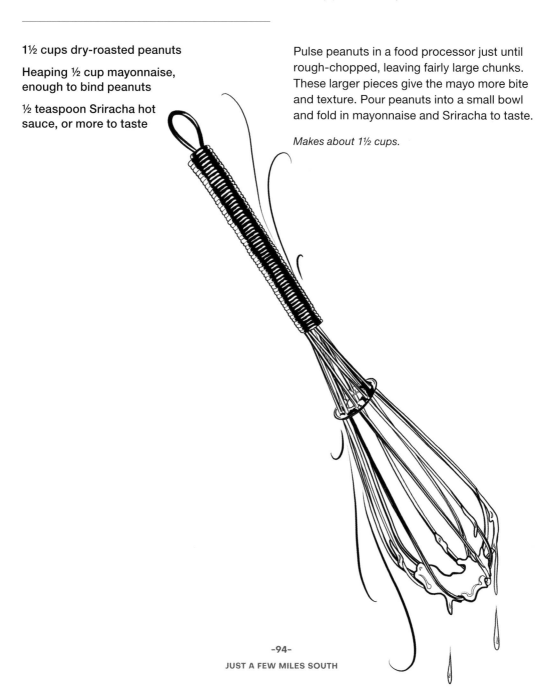

Big Blue Burger

The Big Blue Burger is an homage to the University of Kentucky, where I was national collegiate debate champion. UK men's basketball coach John Calipari once tweeted about having lunch at Wallace Station, and folks started heading over to the restaurant to see if they could catch him there!

Pimiento Blue Cheese was created by Sara Gibbs. Years ago, Wallace Station had a Black and Blue Burger with Cajun spices, blue cheese, and bacon. Sara's spread took the burger to a whole new level.

4 sturdy hamburger buns

4 (6-ounce) burger patties

Pinch Windy Corner Super Spice (see page 166) or favorite grill seasoning

½ cup Bourbon Bacon Jam (recipe follows)

1 cup Pimiento Blue Cheese (see index)

4 thin tomato slices

4 pieces leaf lettuce

Sprinkle both sides of burgers with Windy Corner Super Spice and cook on a grill or in a skillet to the desired temperature.

For each burger: While burgers are cooking, lay out a hamburger bun. Cover the underside of the top with 2–3 tablespoons Bourbon Bacon Jam. Place a burger on the bottom half of the bun and top with a small scoop of Pimiento Blue Cheese, a tomato slice, and a piece of lettuce. Cover with the bun top and serve immediately.

Repeat with remaining ingredients.

Serves 4.

Bourbon Bacon Jam

Bourbon Bacon Jam is used in nearly all our restaurants as an accompaniment to fried oysters or on specialty burgers. Holly Hill Inn executive chef Tyler McNabb created this version. Its roots are in hot bacon vinaigrette, which is used to dress the tender lettuces of early spring. The cooks at Holly Hill Inn prefer a cast-iron skillet for this preparation and low, slow heat.

1 pound thick-sliced bacon, diced small

1 pound sweet yellow onions, diced small

¼ cup whole-grain mustard

½ cup brown sugar, packed

½ cup bourbon

½ cup cider vinegar

Cook bacon in a cast-iron or other heavy skillet over low heat. When completely rendered, pour off some of the grease, add onions, and cook over low heat until onions are caramelized (dark golden brown—the same color as the bacon). Add mustard and warm it in the bacon mixture, then add brown sugar, bourbon, and cider vinegar. The mixture should be dark mahogany brown. Continue to cook over low heat 20–30 minutes until reduced to a jam consistency.

Cool the jam. While still warm, pulse it in a food processor until onions and bacon break up but still have definition. This jam is best when served slightly warm but is also good at room temperature.

Makes about 3 cups.

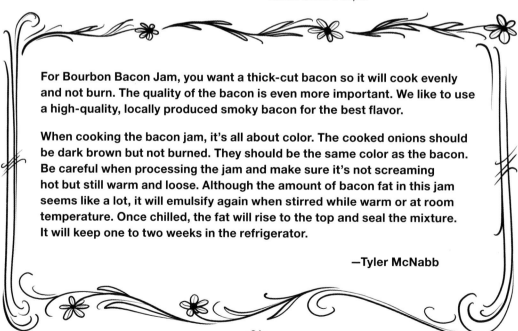

For Bourbon Bacon Jam, you want a thick-cut bacon so it will cook evenly and not burn. The quality of the bacon is even more important. We like to use a high-quality, locally produced smoky bacon for the best flavor.

When cooking the bacon jam, it's all about color. The cooked onions should be dark brown but not burned. They should be the same color as the bacon. Be careful when processing the jam and make sure it's not screaming hot but still warm and loose. Although the amount of bacon fat in this jam seems like a lot, it will emulsify again when stirred while warm or at room temperature. Once chilled, the fat will rise to the top and seal the mixture. It will keep one to two weeks in the refrigerator.

—Tyler McNabb

Casanova Burger

Holly Hill Inn has a multicourse Aphrodisiacs menu on Valentine's Day each year. Wallace Station added its own aphrodisiac burger specials, including the Casanova Burger topped with fried oysters for their reputed effect on the libido. Legend has it that Casanova ate fifty oysters during his morning bath, enjoying them with his lover from the night before.

4 sturdy hamburger buns

4 (6-ounce) burger patties

Salt and pepper for seasoning

½ cup Roasted Garlic Mayonnaise
(recipe follows)

4 slices Pepper Jack cheese

8 fried oysters

4 slices bacon, cooked until crisp

Cook burgers on a grill or in a skillet to the desired temperature, seasoning with salt and pepper.

For each burger: While burgers are cooking, lay out a hamburger bun and slather it with Roasted Garlic Mayonnaise. Add a burger to the bottom half of the bun and cover with a slice of Pepper Jack cheese, 2 fried oysters, and a strip of crisp bacon. Cover with the bun top and serve immediately.

Repeat with remaining ingredients.

Serves 4.

Roasted Garlic Mayonnaise

Roasting garlic softens the cloves, making them spreadable and luscious. Roasting also softens the flavor, resulting in something that barely resembles the sharp, often overwhelming taste of fresh garlic. Our version of the traditional Provençal sauce is less intense but no less flavorful.

1 whole bulb garlic

2 tablespoons olive oil

1 cup mayonnaise

1 teaspoon lemon juice

Salt and pepper to taste

To roast the garlic: Preheat oven to 400 degrees F. Cut ¼ inch off the top of the garlic bulb, exposing the cloves. Peel away any excess papery layers from the outside, leaving the skins of the individual cloves intact. Place in a small baking dish, drizzle with olive oil, and cover with foil. Bake 30–35 minutes, until garlic cloves have softened.

To make the mayonnaise: Cool roasted garlic and squeeze cloves out of the papery skins. Puree garlic and any residual oil in a food processor. Blend all ingredients in a large bowl. Taste for seasoning. Chill at least 1 hour before serving.

Makes 1¼ cups.

Thirty-Seven Burger

In 2015, an American Thoroughbred named American Pharoah won the Triple Crown as well as the Breeders' Cup Classic, together known as the Grand Slam of Thoroughbred racing. American Pharoah was the first Triple Crown winner in thirty-seven years, the last being Affirmed in 1978. This burger was created at Wallace Station in honor of American Pharoah, who now stands at stud at Coolmore America's Ashford Stud Farm, just down the road.

4 sturdy hamburger buns

4 (6-ounce) burger patties

Salt and pepper for seasoning

½ cup Lisa's Remoulade (see index)

4 slices white Cheddar cheese

4 slices Tyler's Fried Green Tomatoes (recipe follows)

½ cup caramelized onions (see index)

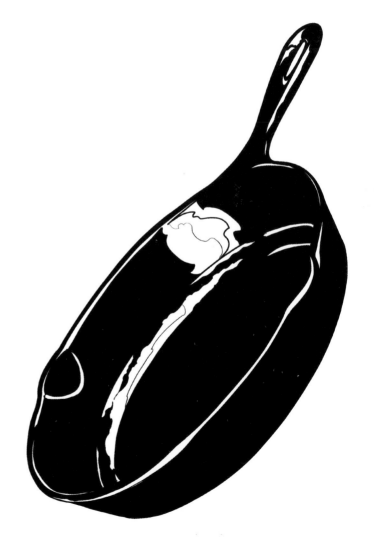

Cook burgers on a grill or in a skillet to the desired temperature, seasoning with salt and pepper.

For each burger: While burgers are cooking, lay out a hamburger bun and slather it with Lisa's Remoulade. Place a burger on the bottom half of the bun and cover with a slice of Cheddar, a fried green tomato slice, and 2 tablespoons caramelized onions. Cover with the bun top and serve immediately.

Repeat with remaining ingredients.

Serves 4.

Tyler's Fried Green Tomatoes

Holly Hill Inn executive chef Tyler McNabb prefers very green tomatoes for frying, with no pink on the inside or outside. Hard green tomatoes make firm slices. Tyler cuts them "pinky wide," resulting in a good amount of tomato flesh, which prevents the slices from drying out. Depending on how they will be used, he fries the slices in canola oil or bacon fat (both work equally well). The fried green tomato is a good garnish for a burger and also makes a great BLT with Roasted Garlic Mayonnaise (see the recipe earlier in this chapter).

4 large, firm green tomatoes, cored and sliced ½- to ¾-inch thick

1 cup buttermilk

¼ cup hot sauce

TYLER'S CORNMEAL DREDGE

½ cup all-purpose flour

½ cup Weisenberger Mill cornmeal

1 teaspoon freshly ground black pepper

1 teaspoon kosher salt

½ teaspoon garlic powder

½ teaspoon onion powder

1 teaspoon ground sweet paprika

Canola oil or rendered bacon fat for frying

Lay sliced tomatoes in a shallow casserole dish. Mix buttermilk and hot sauce and pour over tomatoes. Marinate 1 hour.

Whisk all dredge ingredients together in a medium bowl. Set aside.

Heat canola oil or bacon fat in a large cast-iron skillet over medium-high heat. Lift tomato slices from the buttermilk mixture, coat both sides with the cornmeal mixture, and carefully place in the hot skillet. Don't overcrowd the pan. You want to be able to turn the slices easily without them sticking together. Cook on both sides until dark golden brown, about 3–4 minutes per side. Cook tomato slices in batches, drain, and serve immediately.

Serves 4–6.

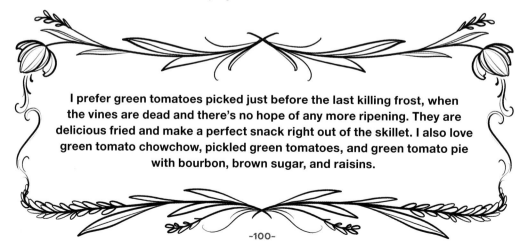

I prefer green tomatoes picked just before the last killing frost, when the vines are dead and there's no hope of any more ripening. They are delicious fried and make a perfect snack right out of the skillet. I also love green tomato chowchow, pickled green tomatoes, and green tomato pie with bourbon, brown sugar, and raisins.

Better Burger Blend

Chef Jonathan Sanning created this burger blend for Smithtown Seafood. Using mushrooms to enhance and stretch the burger mixture makes the protein healthier and more sustainable. This flavorful mixture can be used for any burger or ground beef recipe.

1 tablespoon olive oil

8 ounces sliced button mushrooms

¼ cup finely chopped yellow onion

1 tablespoon minced shallot

½ teaspoon kosher salt

¼ teaspoon freshly ground black pepper

2 roasted garlic cloves, minced (see index)

½ teaspoon minced fresh rosemary

¼ teaspoon minced fresh thyme

1 pound ground beef

Heat olive oil in a nonstick skillet over medium-high heat. Add mushrooms, onion, shallot, salt, and pepper and sauté. Once the mixture begins to cook rapidly, reduce heat to medium and cook, stirring often, 13–15 minutes. The mushrooms will release their liquid, making the mixture very wet, but as they continue to cook, the liquid will be absorbed. At the end of the cooking time, there should be no liquid remaining, and the mixture should stick together.

Remove from heat, toss with roasted garlic and herbs, and cool to room temperature. Place the mushroom mixture in a food processor or mini chopper and pulse until mushrooms are finely minced but still have texture.

In a large bowl, break ground beef into small pieces. Add mushrooms and work the mixture by hand until well blended. Divide into 4 or 5 equal portions and form into patties.

Cook on a grill or in a skillet to the desired temperature.

Serves 4–5.

After attending a seminar offered by the Mushroom Council in Nashville to teach chefs about the Better Burger Project (now the Blended Burger Project), Jonathan Sanning heard a broadcast on public radio about the classic preparation for Beef Wellington. He was inspired to use this traditional dish as the basis for his Beef Wellington Burger—enhanced with duxelles (a sauté of mushrooms, onions or shallots, and herbs) and served on a croissant bun with stout demi-glace, Kenny's Barren County Bleu Cheese, crispy onions, roasted garlic aioli, and microgreens from FoodChain.

Honeywood Hoecake Burger

Former Honeywood chef Josh Smouse boosted the flavor of this burger by using two small "smashed" beef patties to create a sandwich with lots of crisp browned edges. The Cheese Salad, Marinated Cucumbers, and homemade Smoky Ketchup are perfect accompaniments to the richness of the browned beef. Piling all these elements on homemade Weisenberger Mill hoecakes makes this sandwich much more interesting than the typical burger found at backyard barbecues. The Hoecake Burger is best eaten with a fork and knife.

8 (3-ounce) burger patties

Salt and pepper for seasoning

8 (4-inch) Hoecakes (see index)

½ cup Cheese Salad (recipe follows)

12–16 slices Marinated
Cucumbers (recipe follows)

½ cup Smoky Ketchup (recipe follows)

Cook burgers on a grill or in a skillet to the desired temperature, seasoning with salt and pepper. Smash them into thin patties. While burgers are cooking, cook hoecakes on a heated griddle.

For each burger: Place 2 burgers on a hoecake, top with 2 tablespoons Cheese Salad, 3–4 slices Marinated Cucumbers, and 2 tablespoons Smoky Ketchup, and cover with another hoecake. Serve immediately.

Repeat with remaining ingredients.

Serves 4.

Cheese Salad

8 ounces shredded white Cheddar cheese

½ teaspoon granulated garlic

1 teaspoon freshly ground black pepper

1 teaspoon kosher salt

1½ teaspoons Worcestershire sauce

1 cup mayonnaise

Blend all ingredients in a large bowl with a rubber spatula. Chill at least 30 minutes before using.

Makes about 2 cups.

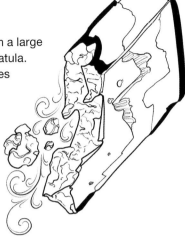

Marinated Cucumbers

1 English cucumber, thinly sliced

¼ cup red wine vinegar

1 tablespoon sugar

1 teaspoon kosher salt

1 teaspoon freshly ground black pepper

Mix all ingredients in a large bowl. Chill at least 30 minutes before using.

Makes about 2 cups.

Smoky Ketchup

1¼ pounds (1½ large) sweet onions, trimmed and sliced

2 tablespoons olive oil

2 tablespoons canola oil

1 tablespoon smoked paprika

1 cup Major Grey's Chutney or other mango chutney

½ cup chili sauce

¼ cup malt vinegar

Sauté onions in both oils over medium heat until softened and golden brown, 12–15 minutes. Remove from heat and cool about 10 minutes. Put onions in a food processor, add remaining ingredients, and puree. Chill before using. Leftovers can be used as a glaze for meatloaf or as a condiment on meatloaf, pork, or turkey sandwiches.

Makes about 3 cups.

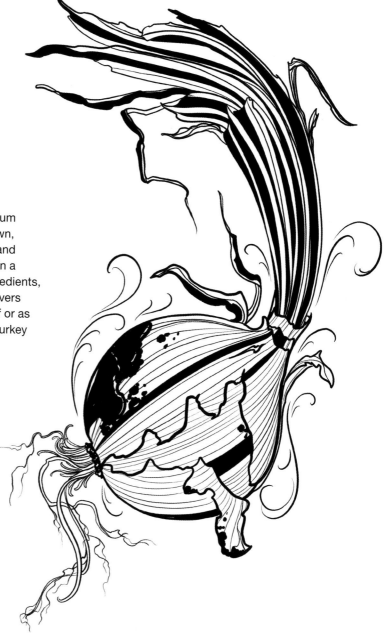

6

Soups, Stews, and Salads

This chapter reminds me of a special patchwork quilt: just like each beautiful square of fabric, each of these recipes takes me back to a special time or place or person. Every one is a winner and has been made thousands of times by many cooks over the years, creating a culinary quilt of sorts that blankets central Kentucky.

SOUPS

Whitesburg Soup Beans

Jared Richardson is one of the most gifted chefs I have ever had the pleasure to work with. At one time, he was also my brother-in-law. When Jared and my sister, Paige, helped me open Wallace Station, he brought many recipes from his hometown of Whitesburg, Kentucky. One of those recipes was for soup beans and cornbread. Soup beans are a staple in Appalachian cooking. They are a nutritious and economical source of protein, easy to make, and delicious with ham hock or salt pork, both of which are readily available in the Appalachian larder. Jared wanted to represent his community on the menu, and this humble, iconic dish was the perfect recipe. Whitesburg Soup Beans and Cornbread remains one of our top-selling items. Wallace Station soup beans were the subject of a short film by Southern Foodways Alliance in 2018 titled *Souped: The Pinto Bean Story*, directed by Ava Lowrey and produced by John T. Edge.

1 pound dried pinto beans

1 cup chopped white onion

5–6 ounces boneless country ham, diced

1½ tablespoons minced garlic

2 teaspoons Worcestershire sauce

2 teaspoons hot sauce

2 teaspoons kosher salt

1 teaspoon freshly ground black pepper

Pick pinto beans for pebbles, rinse until clean, and place in a 4-quart Dutch oven. Cover with cold water and soak 5–6 hours. Drain. Return to the pot, cover beans with about 3 quarts of water, and bring to a boil over medium-high heat.

Add remaining ingredients. Cover and bring to a boil, stirring occasionally. Turn down to a slow simmer and continue to cook until the beans change color and are slightly softened but not mushy, about 2 hours.

Taste for seasoning. Serve with Buttermilk Cornbread or Hoecakes (recipes follow).

Makes 2 quarts. Serves 6.

How did eastern Kentucky get hooked on the pinto bean? Bill Best of Berea, Kentucky, has collected and preserved hundreds of heirloom bean seed varieties over the decades. According to Best, although many varieties of beans were grown throughout central and eastern Kentucky gardens, the pinto bean was cheaper to buy than to grow. During the Depression, when folks were really struggling, pinto beans became a go-to meal for families, especially during the winter (Sheri Castle, "A Helping of Gravy: Soup Beans," *Gravy*, May 19, 2014).

To learn more about heirloom beans or to purchase them, visit Bill Best's website, heirlooms.org. Be sure to read Best's excellent articles about heirloom varieties and Appalachian agriculture.

Buttermilk Cornbread

We bake our cornbread in large cast-iron skillets and then turn it out to cool. The cornbread is cut into wedges and grilled on panini presses to order. Although cornbread is best when eaten right out of the oven, leftovers can be reheated in a skillet or grill pan in a mixture of oil and melted butter. This is a traditional Southern version, made without sugar.

1⅓ cups white or yellow cornmeal

½ cup all-purpose flour

½ teaspoon baking soda

1 teaspoon baking powder

½ teaspoon iodized salt

1 large egg, beaten

1⅓ cups buttermilk

2 tablespoons unsalted butter, melted

1 tablespoon butter or bacon drippings

Place a 9-inch cast-iron skillet in the oven and preheat to 400 degrees F.

In a medium bowl, mix together cornmeal, flour, baking soda, baking powder, and salt. Add egg, buttermilk, and melted butter and mix well with a whisk.

Carefully remove the hot cast-iron skillet from the oven and drop in 1 tablespoon butter or bacon drippings, swirl quickly to coat the pan, and return to the oven for another 2–3 minutes, until the butter bubbles and turns dark golden brown. Remove the skillet from the oven again and pour in the batter. Return immediately to the oven and bake 18–23 minutes, until the edges are brown and the center is firm to the touch. Cut into 12 wedges. Serve immediately with butter and/or Whitesburg Soup Beans.

Makes 1 large skillet bread or 12 wedges.

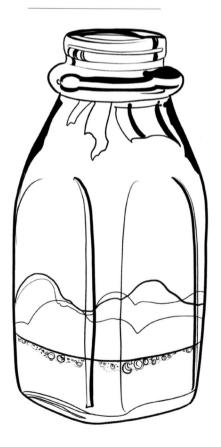

Hoecakes

Hoecakes are thin pancakes made with a batter of cornmeal, baking powder, salt, and water or milk. Some folks add a little flour, an egg, or buttermilk—the variations are endless. This recipe calls for self-rising cornmeal, but if you don't have any on hand, add ½ teaspoon iodized salt and 1 tablespoon baking powder to 1 cup cornmeal.

1 cup self-rising Weisenberger Mill cornmeal

1 tablespoon all-purpose flour

1 tablespoon sugar

1 large egg, beaten

1 cup buttermilk

Whisk cornmeal, flour, and sugar in a small bowl. Add egg and buttermilk and whisk well to combine. The mixture should be pourable. Let batter rest about 10 minutes.

Heat an electric skillet to 350 degrees F, or place a nonstick skillet over medium heat. Pour or ladle batter onto the heated surface and cook until golden brown on both sides.

Makes about 1¾ cups batter: 14 small (3-inch) hoecakes or 7 large (6-inch) hoecakes.

All hoecakes are variations of corn pone. Around these parts, corn pone is thought of as cornbread batter baked in a round skillet or round cake pan. A hoecake is smaller and cooked in a skillet or on a griddle. The kitchen staff at Wallace Station makes big, thick corn pones in cast-iron skillets each day, and hoecakes are griddled each day at Windy Corner Market, Honeywood, and Zim's. The big ones are a delicious accompaniment to soup beans, and the little silver-dollar-size ones are used for canapés. Honeywood created a Hoecake Burger, sandwiching two thin patties and our Cheese Salad between two hoecakes (see the recipe in chapter 5). Delicious!

Creamy Chicken and Mushroom Soup

This recipe was created to use leftover fried chicken. Our cooks would remove the crispy outer coating, pull the meat from the bones, and chop it up. Eventually, the dish became so popular that they had to poach extra chicken just for the soup. The flavor profile is similar to that of a good Kentucky cook's fried chicken, with herbs and a little spice. Both white and dark meat work just fine.

2 tablespoons olive oil

1½ cups diced carrots

1½ cups diced yellow onions

1 pound button mushrooms, cleaned and chopped

4 tablespoons (½ stick) unsalted butter

½ cup all-purpose flour

1½ quarts chicken broth, warm

½ teaspoon dried thyme

2 teaspoons ground sage

1½ teaspoons kosher salt

¾ teaspoon freshly ground black pepper

2 cups half-and-half

3 cups diced cooked chicken

Salt and freshly ground pepper to taste

Heat olive oil over medium heat in a 4-quart Dutch oven. Add carrots, onions, and mushrooms and sauté about 4 minutes or until vegetables begin to soften and brown. Cover, reduce heat to medium-low, and sweat 3 minutes. Uncover, increase heat to medium, add butter, and stir until melted. Stir in flour. Cook 2 minutes, stirring constantly so the vegetable mixture doesn't scorch but the flour cooks.

Add warm broth and whisk rapidly to prevent lumps from forming. Be sure to scrape the bottom of the pan. Add thyme, sage, salt, and pepper and cook over medium-high heat until the soup starts to thicken. Reduce to a simmer, cover, and cook gently 20–25 minutes. Whisk often, or the roux will settle and burn.

Add half-and-half and cooked chicken and bring to a gentle simmer. Cook, stirring often, another 5 minutes. Taste and season with salt and pepper. Serve immediately.

Makes about 3 quarts. Serves 6–8.

Smithtown Seafood Clam Chowder

Smithtown Seafood's clam chowder recipe was developed by chef Jonathan Sanning. Michael Blowen, of Old Friends Thoroughbred Retirement Farm in nearby Scott County, claims it is the best clam chowder outside of Boston. And as a Beantown native, he should know!

4 strips bacon, stacked and cut crosswise in thin strips

½ cup small-diced yellow onion

1 rib celery, small diced (about ½ cup)

1 shallot, minced

3 cloves roasted garlic or fresh garlic, chopped

4 tablespoons (½ stick) unsalted butter

½ teaspoon dried whole-leaf thyme

1 bay leaf

½ teaspoon freshly ground black pepper

⅓ cup all-purpose flour

1 quart clam juice (use some from the chopped ocean clams below)

1 cup heavy cream

1 cup whole milk

1 tablespoon fresh lemon juice

4 cups peeled and small-diced potatoes (about 2 large russet potatoes)

20 ounces chopped ocean clams or whole baby clams

Kosher salt to taste

Heat a large, heavy stockpot over medium heat. Add bacon and sauté briefly until bacon begins to cook and render. Add onion, celery, and shallot and sauté until bacon fat is rendered and vegetables begin to soften. Add garlic, butter, thyme, bay leaf, and black pepper. When butter is melted, add flour and cook 2 minutes, stirring often. Add 1 cup clam juice and stir until the mixture thickens. Repeat until all the clam juice has been incorporated. Add cream, milk, lemon juice, potatoes, and clams and bring to a simmer. Reduce heat to medium-low and lightly simmer, stirring often, until potatoes are tender, about 20 minutes. Season with salt to taste.

Makes about 3 quarts. Serves 8–10.

Canned chopped ocean clams or whole baby clams can be found in most grocery stores. The size of the can varies—from 6½ ounces for chopped ocean clams to 10 ounces for whole baby clams. If you are lucky enough to have access to fresh clams, clean them carefully to remove any bits of shell, chop fine, and add 2–2½ cups to chowder.

Holly Hill Inn Butternut Squash Bisque

Good homemade chicken stock is the key to this soup. Canned chicken broth is too light to bring out the flavors of the roasted vegetables and sweet fruit juices, so wait until you have rich stock on hand before trying this recipe.

2 tablespoons unsalted butter

2 cups diced sweet onion

2 tablespoons minced garlic

2 teaspoons peeled minced ginger root

10 cups rich, homemade chicken stock

2 cups peeled diced russet potatoes

1 cup peeled diced pear or apple

8 cups roasted butternut squash, peeled and diced (about 5 pounds, see note below)

1 cup heavy cream

½ cup orange juice or apple cider

2 tablespoons lemon juice

1 teaspoon Louisiana-style hot sauce

Kosher salt to taste

¼ teaspoon ground nutmeg

Pinch cayenne pepper

¼ teaspoon ground cinnamon

Crème fraîche or sour cream and toasted pumpkin seeds for garnish

Melt butter in a large stockpot over medium heat. Add onion, garlic, and ginger and sauté briefly. Lower heat, cover, and sweat the vegetables until they have softened, about 10 minutes. Add chicken stock, potatoes, and pear or apple. Increase heat to medium-high and bring to a simmer. Cook until potatoes and fruit are soft, about 10 minutes.

Stir in roasted butternut squash and simmer briefly to combine. Puree with an immersion blender, then strain through a fine mesh sieve.

Return strained soup to the pot over low heat. Add cream, orange juice or apple cider, lemon juice, hot sauce, and spices. Taste for seasoning.

Garnish with crème fraîche or sour cream and toasted pumpkin seeds.

Makes 1 gallon. Serves 8–10 as a meal or 16 as a starter.

Note: To roast butternut squash, preheat oven to 400 degrees F. Halve the squash lengthwise, scrape out seeds, and place on a baking sheet, cut side down. Cover with foil and seal. Bake 1 hour or longer, depending on size, until a knife easily pierces the skin and flesh of the squash. Cool until easy enough to handle.

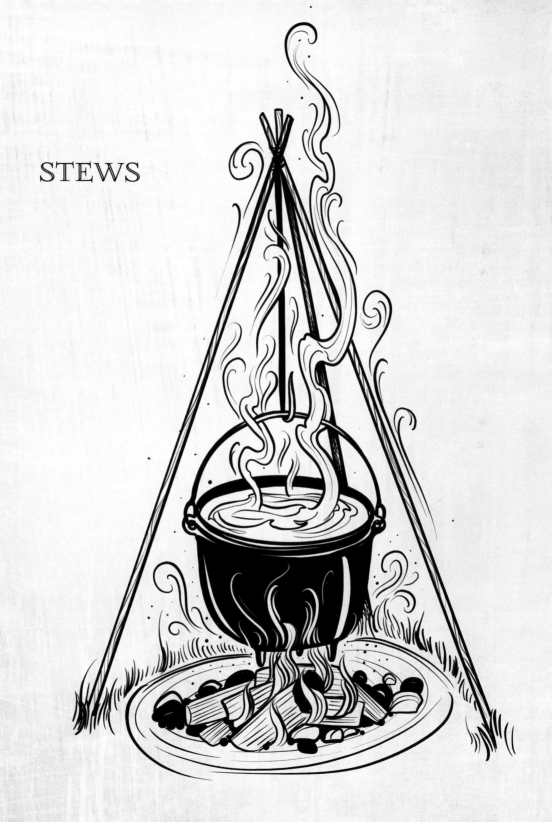

STEWS

Wallace Station Burgoo

This recipe was inspired by my friend and burgoo master Rick Caudle of Midway, who was featured in the 2008 documentary *Burgoo! Legendary Stew of the South*. This is not a "chef" recipe; it is a down-home, authentic burgoo. I have cooked deconstructed burgoos with squab, lamb, beef, and demi-glace, but I love Rick's version the best. His burgoo, which he learned to make from legendary "Burgoo King" Jim Conway of Frankfort, Kentucky, is simple and well seasoned—just meats and vegetables cooked together over low heat for a long time until they melt into each other. I've seen pictures of burgoos online, and here's a hint: If the burgoo looks really pretty in a bowl, it's not authentic. You want all the ingredients to simmer down to one good-tasting blend.

2–3 pounds chicken leg quarters

1 quart chicken broth

3–4 pounds beef chuck roast, cut into stew-size pieces, about 1 inch

3–4 pounds pork shoulder or butt, cut into stew-size pieces, about 1 inch

2–3 quarts water or chicken broth

1 cup dried great northern beans, soaked at least 1 hour

1 cup green beans, cut into 1-inch pieces (fresh or canned)

2 large russet potatoes, peeled and diced

1 cup small-diced onion

1 cup small-diced carrot

½ cup small-diced celery

1 cup small-diced turnip

1 cup frozen peas

1 cup corn (fresh or frozen)

1 (14½-ounce) can diced tomatoes

2 cups tomato vegetable juice cocktail

½ cup mild steak sauce

¼–½ cup hot pepper sauce

½ cup Worcestershire sauce

Salt and pepper to taste

Cover chicken in chicken broth and simmer until tender, 45 minutes or longer, depending on size. Reserve the broth, pull the meat from the bones, and set aside in the refrigerator.

Add beef and pork to a large, heavy-bottomed kettle (at least 8 quarts). Cover with water or broth and bring to a simmer, skimming any foam that forms on the surface. Simmer over low heat 1 hour or until the meat is fairly tender.

Add soaked great northern beans and green beans and continue to simmer for another hour.

Add chicken meat and reserved chicken broth. Add vegetables and tomato vegetable juice cocktail, steak sauce, and hot sauce. Simmer another 1½–2 hours. Keep the heat low, and stir now and then to prevent sticking, adding scant amounts of water or broth as needed. The vegetables and meat should cook into each other, forming a thick mixture. Add Worcestershire sauce, salt, and pepper to taste.

Makes almost 2 gallons. Serves 16–20.

Burgoo can also be finished in a slow cooker. Mix the cooked chicken and meats and the vegetables and seasonings in a large bowl and then pour into an 8-quart slow cooker or two 4- to 6-quart slow cookers. Add enough reserved broth to cover three-quarters of the vegetables and simmer on low 6–8 hours or until the vegetables are tender. Season with salt to taste.

Rick Caudle's burgoo roots are deep. In the 1930s, his uncle Frank Watts would invite his male friends to camp at the Kentucky River for a week of fishing and probably bourbon drinking. On the last day, they'd make a burgoo. Jim Conway picked up the tradition when he returned from the service in 1947 or 1948. Jim, Rick's dad, Shirley Caudle, and his uncle Jub Caudle would make a burgoo in the fall after housing tobacco. They took a lard can, lit a fire under an old beech tree, and started a burgoo friendship that continues in their families to this day. They cooked burgoos at the distilleries along Glenn's Creek, including Labrot and Graham (now Woodford Reserve) and the Crow's Nest at Old Crow. Eventually, they moved their burgoo cooking to Rick's camp called Seven Creeks.

After Rick returned from serving in the US Navy, he graduated from eating the stew to learning how to make it from Jim Conway. Until Jim's death in 2001, he and Rick prepared burgoos for the annual VFW Fourth of July celebration, the 200th anniversary of the Kentucky capitol, and, since 1981, the annual Millville Hillbilly Daze. Rick's cousin Tony Wash is his helper these days. They still go to Seven Creeks every year with their buddies, continuing a decades-long tradition of fishing and cooking a camp burgoo the old-fashioned way: in a cast-iron kettle over a wood fire with fresh-caught game.

Rick's burgoo follows Jim's traditional recipe, which yields about 25 gallons. At camp, Rick uses squirrel, rabbit, dove breast, and venison in his burgoo. When he makes burgoo for groups in town, he leaves out the game and cooks over propane. He calls it "CityGoo."

Bourbon Trail Chili

This chili was created by Sara Gibbs for Glenn's Creek Café at Woodford Reserve Distillery (she often checked up on the cooks to make sure they weren't altering her recipe). Using local ground beef, bourbon-smoked paprika, and Kentucky bourbon, this is a Kentucky Proud dish. It contains several flavor notes from the bourbon flavor wheel (herbal, citrus, wood, and spice). The chili can be served in a bowl, over tortilla chips with garnishes, or as the main component of Sara's Hoot 'n Holler Taco Salad, composed of chopped iceberg lettuce, tomatoes, Cheddar cheese, chopped onions, sour cream, and salty corn chips.

1½ pounds ground beef

Salt and pepper for seasoning

1 tablespoon olive oil

2½ teaspoons minced garlic

1 teaspoon dried oregano

1 teaspoon dried ground sage

1 medium onion, diced (about 2 cups)

2 green bell peppers, diced

½ cup orange juice

3 tablespoons chili powder

2 teaspoons Bourbon Barrel Foods bourbon-smoked paprika (see page 167) or other smoked paprika

2 teaspoons ground cumin

2 teaspoons minced chipotle pepper in adobo

1 teaspoon kosher salt

1 (28-ounce) can crushed tomatoes

3 cups water

1 (15½-ounce) can black beans, well drained

1 (15½-ounce) can great northern beans, well drained

½ cup bourbon

Sour cream, shredded Cheddar, thinly sliced green onions for garnish

Brown ground beef in a 4-quart Dutch oven and season lightly with salt and pepper. Drain off excess fat and set meat aside.

Add olive oil to the pan, then add garlic, oregano, sage, onion, and bell peppers. Sauté over medium heat until vegetables begin to soften, about 4–5 minutes.

Deglaze with orange juice, then add chili powder, smoked paprika, cumin, chipotles, salt, and tomatoes. Bring to a simmer. Stir in water, beans, and browned meat. Simmer 15 minutes. Add bourbon and simmer another 15–20 minutes until the proper consistency is achieved. Taste for seasoning.

Garnish with sour cream, shredded Cheddar, and green onions.

Makes about 2½ quarts. Serves 6–8.

Arugula

Tango

Red Oak
lettuce

Spinach

Mizuna

Romaine

Chard

SALADS

Wallace Station Red Bliss Potato Salad

My sister, Paige, created this stripped-down potato salad for opening day at Wallace Station. The key is using high-quality mayonnaise and not letting the potatoes get ice cold before dressing them. If the potatoes are slightly warm, they will absorb the dressing, making them more flavorful. We sell gallons of this simple salad every day. It's easy to make and easy to eat!

3 pounds small red-skinned potatoes, scrubbed and eyes removed

1½ teaspoons kosher salt

1 cup finely chopped celery

1 cup finely chopped red onion

3 tablespoons Dijon mustard

2 cups mayonnaise

1 tablespoon water

Salt and freshly ground black pepper to taste

Place potatoes in a small stockpot and cover with cold water. Bring to a boil. Simmer about 13 minutes, or until potatoes are tender when pierced with a knife. Drain and cool slightly.

Cut potatoes in a medium dice, add remaining ingredients, and mix thoroughly. Taste for seasoning. Chill at least 30 minutes before serving.

Makes 2 quarts. Serves 12–16.

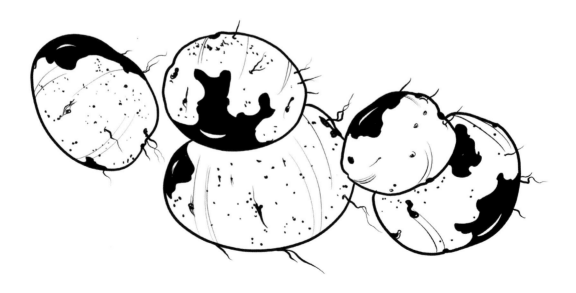

1812 Potato Salad

Created by Sara Gibbs for Woodford Reserve Distillery's bicentennial celebration in 2012, this salad was served at Glenn's Creek Café as part of a special weeklong menu. Its old-fashioned, vinegar-marinated style is reminiscent of Kentucky's early culinary history. The salad keeps well at room temperature, since it is less dependent on refrigeration than a mayonnaise-based salad.

2 pounds red-skinned potatoes, scrubbed and eyes removed, ½-inch dice

1 cup diced celery

4 green onions, thinly sliced

¼ cup minced fresh parsley

DRESSING

3 tablespoons red wine vinegar

1 garlic clove, minced

1 teaspoon dried oregano

1 teaspoon kosher salt

½ teaspoon freshly ground black pepper

2 tablespoons olive oil

2 tablespoons canola oil

Mix dressing ingredients in a small bowl. Set aside.

Cook potatoes until tender, about 10 minutes. Drain and cool slightly, then toss with dressing. Cool to room temperature and allow mixture to marinate. The potatoes will soak up most, if not all, of the liquid.

Add celery, green onion, and parsley and toss well. Reseason with salt and pepper. Serve at room temperature or chilled. It will keep at least 4 days in the refrigerator.

Makes almost 2 quarts. Serves 12–16.

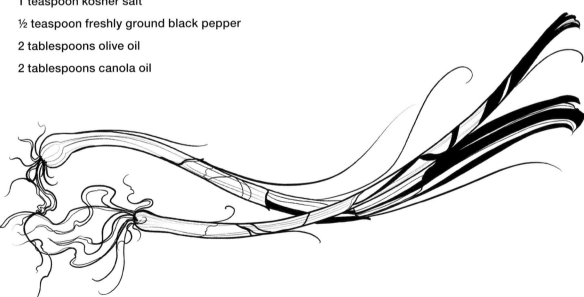

Creamy Coleslaw

Creamy Coleslaw is one of Wallace Station's original recipes and is still served there daily, as well as at several of our other restaurants. The dressing is based on my Grandma Zim's recipe.

1 (16-ounce) package coleslaw mix with carrots (or ¾ pound shredded cabbage plus 1 shredded carrot)

¼ cup thinly sliced red onion

DRESSING

1 cup mayonnaise

2 tablespoons cider vinegar

1 tablespoon sugar

1 teaspoon kosher salt

½ teaspoon ground sweet paprika

¼ teaspoon white pepper

In a medium bowl, mix dressing ingredients until thoroughly blended. Add shredded vegetables and toss lightly.

Taste for seasoning and adjust if necessary. Chill.

Makes about 1 quart. Serves 6–8.

Sassy Sorghum Slaw

Bourbon Sorghum Vinaigrette makes this colorful dish unique and memorable. The slaw is best when eaten the day it is made for the most flavor and crunch. However, the vegetables can be prepared ahead of time, tossed with black pepper, and stored in the refrigerator. When you're ready to serve, just add the salt and the dressing.

1 (16-ounce) package coleslaw mix with carrots (or ¾ pound shredded cabbage plus 1 shredded carrot)

1 cup red cabbage, thinly sliced

½ yellow bell pepper, julienned

2 ribs celery, thinly sliced

½ cup red onion, thinly sliced

1 teaspoon kosher salt

½ teaspoon freshly ground black pepper

⅓ cup Bourbon Sorghum Vinaigrette (recipe follows)

Toss prepared vegetables with salt and pepper in a large bowl. Add Bourbon Sorghum Vinaigrette and toss gently. Taste for seasoning and serve immediately.

Makes about 1 quart. Serves 6–8.

Bourbon Sorghum Vinaigrette

Leftover vinaigrette is a treasure to have in the refrigerator. You can use it as a marinade for grilled chicken, a dressing for lettuce salads featuring fruit and cheese, or a dressing for grain salads with dried fruit (see Pam's Healthy Grain Salad later in this chapter).

1 cup malt vinegar

2 teaspoons kosher salt

½ teaspoon ground sweet paprika

½ teaspoon dry mustard

Dash Crystal hot sauce or other Louisiana-style hot sauce

1 tablespoon grated onion

10 tablespoons sorghum

2 tablespoons bourbon

1 cup canola oil

In a large bowl, whisk together vinegar, salt, paprika, mustard, hot sauce, and grated onion. Warm sorghum in a microwave on medium power to loosen it, then stir into vinegar mixture along with bourbon.

Add oil slowly and emulsify, whisking constantly.

Makes about 2½ cups.

The National Society of Colonial Dames in the Commonwealth of Kentucky owns, preserves, and maintains the Orlando Brown House in Frankfort. It was built in 1835 and designed by Gideon Shryock, thought to be Kentucky's first native-born architect and designer of the Old State Capitol in Frankfort. For several years running, our catering team has prepared a historic Kentucky dinner in the house as a fund-raiser for the Dames. A few of the Brown family recipes have been handed down in community cookbooks over the years, including a maple syrup dressing. I used that recipe as inspiration for my Bourbon Sorghum Vinaigrette, replacing the maple syrup with Kentucky's native sorghum and finishing it with a shot of Woodford Reserve bourbon. The dressing has become a favorite and was served regularly at Woodford Reserve Distillery on our Bourbon Academy Salad of Bibb lettuce, sliced oranges, candied pecans, and thin-sliced red onion.

Black Bean and Corn Salad

Chef Cameron Roszkowski created this dish when Windy Corner Market opened, and it is still on the menu. Although this salad can be made year-round using frozen corn, it is especially good in midsummer using fresh local corn cut from the cob. It is the perfect choice for a summer potluck or barbecue.

2 (15-ounce) cans black beans, drained and rinsed

1 (12-ounce) bag frozen corn kernels, cooked according to package directions, or 6 ears fresh corn, boiled 5 minutes and cut from the cob

LIME VINAIGRETTE

½ small orange, juiced (¼ cup juice)

1 tablespoon lime juice

1 tablespoon cider vinegar

½ jalapeño, seeded and minced (about 1½ tablespoons)

½ teaspoon minced garlic

¼ teaspoon freshly ground black pepper

1 teaspoon kosher salt

1 teaspoon ground cumin

Pinch cayenne pepper

½ teaspoon chili powder

¼ cup rough-chopped cilantro leaves

¼ cup canola oil

1 cup grape tomatoes, sliced in half

½ large yellow bell pepper, julienned

½ cup small-diced red onion

Place black beans and corn in a large bowl. Set aside.

To make vinaigrette, place orange juice, lime juice, vinegar, jalapeño, garlic, seasonings, and cilantro in a blender. Blend while drizzling in oil.

Add vinaigrette to the bean and corn mixture and mix well. Add grape tomatoes, bell peppers, and red onions and toss gently until well combined. Taste for seasoning.

Makes 1½ quarts. Serves 10–12.

Pam's Healthy Grain Salad

My mother, Pam Sexton, was a great cook and especially loved her whole grains and dark leafy greens. She often made a seven-grain pilaf for dinner and would turn the leftovers into a grain salad the next day. Her pilaf contained brown rice, wild rice, millet, wheat berries, bulgur, quinoa, and barley. That mix was a little cumbersome for the small Windy Corner kitchen, so I shortened the list, but the salad is still a tribute to my mom. The variety of grains makes this salad protein rich and texturally interesting. This blend is the Windy Corner staff's favorite, but substitutions such as farro, rye berries, or sorghum work equally well.

½ cup wheat berries

½ cup millet

½ cup bulgur

½ cup quinoa

½ cup wild rice

2 ribs celery, diced (about ¾ cup)

¾ cup shredded carrots

½ cup diced red onion

¾ cup dried cranberries

1 cup Bourbon Sorghum Vinaigrette (see earlier in this chapter)

Salt and pepper to taste

Cook each grain separately according to package directions. Cool to room temperature.

Stir all ingredients together in a large bowl. Mix well. Chill at least 30 minutes before serving. Taste for seasoning.

Makes a little over 2 quarts. Serves 12–16.

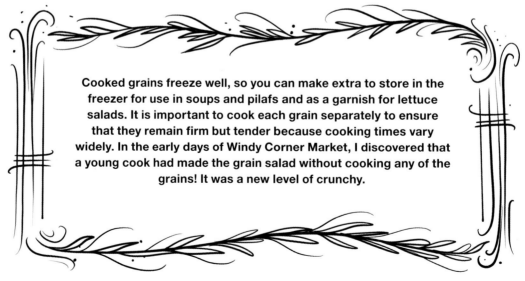

Cooked grains freeze well, so you can make extra to store in the freezer for use in soups and pilafs and as a garnish for lettuce salads. It is important to cook each grain separately to ensure that they remain firm but tender because cooking times vary widely. In the early days of Windy Corner Market, I discovered that a young cook had made the grain salad without cooking any of the grains! It was a new level of crunchy.

Lisa's Orzo Salad

When Windy Corner Market opened in 2010, one of the investors insisted that this pasta salad be part of the menu. Created by Lisa Laufer at Holly Hill Inn, it is now a beloved menu item at several of our restaurants. Orzo salad is good at room temperature and is an excellent choice for a summer picnic.

8 ounces dry orzo pasta, cooked al dente

½ cup (about 2 ounces) chopped sun-dried tomatoes

1 (6-ounce) jar marinated artichoke hearts, drained and chopped

½ cup pitted kalamata olives, chopped

¼ cup minced fresh parsley

2 green onions, thinly sliced

½ cup crumbled Feta cheese

½ cup Lemon Oregano Vinaigrette (recipe follows)

In a large bowl, toss cooked orzo with sun-dried tomatoes, artichoke hearts, olives, parsley, green onions, and Feta cheese. Whisk vinaigrette and pour over pasta mixture. Mix well with a rubber spatula. This salad is best served at room temperature.

Makes about 5 cups.
Serves 8–10.

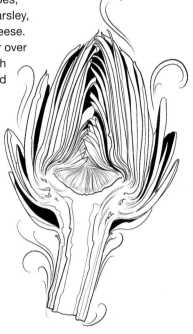

Lemon Oregano Vinaigrette

¼ cup fresh lemon juice

½ teaspoon kosher salt

¼ teaspoon freshly ground black pepper

½ teaspoon dry mustard

½ teaspoon dried oregano

½ cup canola oil

¼ cup olive oil

Place all ingredients except oils in a food processor. Pulse to combine. With the processor running, slowly drizzle in the oils. Taste for seasoning. Chill 30 minutes before using.

Makes about 1 cup.

Jonathan's Nebbe Black-Eyed Pea Salad

This colorful protein-rich salad is the brainchild of former Smithtown Seafood chef Jonathan Sanning. His version of the Senegalese classic *saladu nebbe* is best served at room temperature and is a good side dish for alfresco dining. This recipe is a healthy alternative to meat-heavy black-eyed pea dishes served for good luck on New Year's Day.

1 pound dried black-eyed peas or 4 (15-ounce) cans, drained and rinsed

½ cup lime juice

1 cup minced parsley

1 tablespoon kosher salt

1½ teaspoons freshly ground black pepper

1 habanero pepper, seeded and finely minced

1 cup canola oil

6 green onions, sliced thinly (use green and white parts), about 1 cup

1½ roasted red bell peppers, small diced, about ¾ cup

1 English cucumber, small diced

1 pint (2 cups) quartered cherry tomatoes or halved grape tomatoes

Boil dried black-eyed peas until tender but not mushy. Salt heavily. Let them sit 2 minutes, then drain and set aside.

Combine lime juice, parsley, salt, pepper, and habanero in a food processor and drizzle in oil.

Combine black-eyed peas, green onions, red bell peppers, cucumbers, and tomatoes in a bowl and toss with the lime and herb mixture. Taste for seasoning.

Makes about 11 cups. Serves 12–16.

LETTUCE SALADS
AND DRESSINGS

Kentucky is a garden of gorgeous lettuce almost year-round. Spring is best, when restaurants have access to a huge variety of greens. The supply dwindles in summer if we have soaring temperatures and a dry spell or in the dead of winter if temperatures plunge. Some growers use cold frames to ensure a winter lettuce supply.

Smithtown Seafood is lucky to have year-round lettuce grown outside its back door at the FoodChain urban farm. FoodChain raises lettuce in long growing beds as part of a nonprofit aquaponics project. Smithtown Seafood makes every effort to use locally grown lettuce in all its salads. As the business has grown, Smithtown has expanded its lineup of suppliers to include Crooked Row Farm in Fayette County and Salad Days in Woodford County, among others.

Salad is important to me because making salad was my first job in the kitchen with my mother. We made a big salad every night for dinner, using her wooden salad bowl. She even wrote a poem about salad, and it hangs above table 31 at Holly Hill Inn.

Low-Carb Protein Power Chef Salad

High-protein salads were popular when Wallace Station opened, so this salad has had a presence on the menu from the beginning. Sliced deli meats can be used, but leftover home-roasted ham or turkey is even better. The deli meats used at Wallace Station are high quality, low sodium, and low fat. We especially like this salad with Penny's Pumpkinseed Vinaigrette for an extra punch of protein, but Creamy Blue Cheese is another, more decadent option.

12 cups mixed lettuce (romaine, spring mix, and/or spinach)

½ cup shredded red or green cabbage

½ cup shredded carrots

1 cup Penny's Pumpkinseed Vinaigrette or Creamy Blue Cheese Dressing (recipes follow)

8 ounces roasted turkey breast, chopped

8 ounces city ham, chopped

6 ounces Swiss cheese, cut in thin strips

Thinly sliced red onion rings

1 cup grape tomato halves

2 ounces alfalfa or other fresh sprouts

4 hard-cooked eggs, sliced or quartered

In a large bowl, mix lettuce, cabbage, and carrots.

For each serving: Place 2 large handfuls (about 3 cups) lettuce mix in a medium bowl, add 2 ounces of dressing, and toss together gently with salad tongs. Mound dressed greens on a large plate or in a shallow bowl and garnish with 2 ounces turkey, 2 ounces ham, 1½ ounces Swiss cheese, several red onion rings, ¼ cup grape tomato halves, a pinch of fresh

sprouts, and a sliced or quartered hard-cooked egg.

Repeat with remaining ingredients.

Serves 4.

Penny's Pumpkinseed Vinaigrette

My family's salad tradition included Mom's pumpkinseed vinaigrette. She made it in the blender every week and kept it in a small Ball jar in the fridge. It is one of my favorite recipes of hers. When she was a girl, her nickname was Penny, so I gave this dressing the same nickname—my secret tribute to my mom and her good taste. So thick you can stand a fork in it, Penny's Pumpkinseed Vinaigrette also makes a delicious dip for crudités or dressing for cut cabbage.

½ cup red wine vinegar

4 cloves garlic, minced

1 tablespoon Dijon mustard

1 teaspoon freshly ground black pepper

2 teaspoons sugar

1 teaspoon kosher salt

1 cup toasted pumpkin seeds

1½ cups olive oil (or 1 cup olive oil and ½ cup canola oil)

¼ cup water (optional)

In a blender or food processor, process vinegar, garlic, Dijon, black pepper, sugar, salt, and pumpkin seeds until a puree forms. With the equipment running, drizzle in oil and process until dressing is emulsified and smooth. If it seems too thick, add up to ¼ cup tepid water until the preferred consistency is achieved.

Makes 2½ cups.

Creamy Blue Cheese Dressing

2 cups mayonnaise

½ cup blue cheese crumbles

2 teaspoons Worcestershire sauce

1½ teaspoons hot sauce

¼ teaspoon white pepper

¼ teaspoon kosher salt

1 teaspoon fresh lemon juice

2 tablespoons sour cream

½ teaspoon garlic powder

Whisk ingredients in a small bowl until incorporated. Taste for seasoning.

Chill at least 30 minutes before serving. Store in a container with a tight-fitting lid.

Makes 2¾ cups.

Super Foods Salad

Garbanzo beans, pumpkin seeds, tofu, and tahini (in the dressing) provide plant-based protein in this hearty vegetarian dinner salad. When locally grown cucumbers are out of season, we like to use the English hothouse variety, leaving the skin on. On the menu, this salad is paired with Balsamic Miso Vinaigrette, but Jonathan's Ginger-Soy Vinaigrette (recipe follows) is a nice alternative, especially when substituting edamame for garbanzo beans.

12 cups mixed lettuce (romaine and baby greens)

½ cup shredded red or green cabbage

½ cup shredded carrots

1 cup Balsamic Miso Vinaigrette (recipe follows)

1⅓ cups cooked garbanzo beans, rinsed if canned

8 radishes, thinly sliced

1⅓ cups sliced cucumbers

¼ cup toasted pumpkin seeds

12 ounces Fried Tofu (see index)

In a large bowl, mix lettuce, cabbage, and carrots.

For each serving: Place 2 large handfuls lettuce mix (about 3 cups) in a medium bowl, add ¼ cup vinaigrette, and toss gently with salad tongs. Mound dressed greens on a large plate or in a shallow bowl and garnish with ⅓ cup garbanzo beans, 2 sliced radishes, ⅓ cup sliced cucumbers, pumpkin seeds, and 10–12 cubes tofu.

Repeat with remaining ingredients.

Serves 4.

Balsamic Miso Vinaigrette

The funny thing about this dressing is that it has no miso in it. I'm not sure how it got the name. The secret ingredients are tahini and soy sauce. It is one of the first recipes I ever made in a professional kitchen (at the Health Pub), and it remains one of my favorites. It has been on the menu everywhere I've ever been a chef.

2 tablespoons whole-grain mustard

2 tablespoons tahini

2 tablespoons soy sauce

1 garlic clove, sliced

½ cup balsamic vinegar

¼ teaspoon freshly ground black pepper

1½ cups salad oil

Place all ingredients except oil in a food processor and pulse until combined. Slowly drizzle in oil to create an emulsion. Taste for seasoning. Chill at least 30 minutes before using.

Makes about 2½ cups.

In 1987, I landed my first restaurant job in New York City at the Health Pub, a great macrobiotic restaurant on Twenty-Second Street and Second Avenue. No meat or dairy products were served or used in the cooking there. We milled our own flour, and every menu item as well as the menu proper was in balance according to macrobiotic principles. At the Health Pub, one of the top-selling items was a plate full of delicious steamed vegetables, and most people ordered the Balsamic Miso Vinaigrette for dipping. I now serve steamed vegetable baskets at Windy Corner Market and Zim's Café.

Jonathan's Ginger-Soy Vinaigrette

Spiked with fresh ginger and lime juice, this dressing was created for Smithtown Seafood's Singapore Salad, but it will enhance any noodle or lettuce salad.

1 tablespoon peeled minced fresh ginger root

1½ teaspoons minced garlic

1 tablespoon chili garlic sauce

2 tablespoons white vinegar

⅓ cup unseasoned rice vinegar

2 tablespoons fresh lime juice

½ cup soy sauce

¼ cup sugar

¼ teaspoon salt

⅔ cup canola oil

Place ginger root, garlic, and chili garlic sauce in the bowl of a mini chopper and process until a paste forms. Add vinegars and lime juice and process until well mixed. Pour mixture into a medium bowl and whisk in soy sauce, sugar, and salt. Drizzle in oil, whisking constantly. Store in a container with a tight-fitting lid and shake well before using.

Makes about 2 cups.

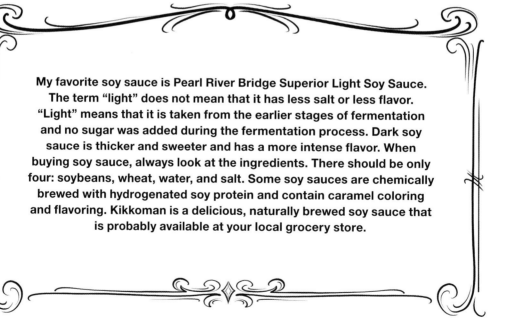

My favorite soy sauce is Pearl River Bridge Superior Light Soy Sauce. The term "light" does not mean that it has less salt or less flavor. "Light" means that it is taken from the earlier stages of fermentation and no sugar was added during the fermentation process. Dark soy sauce is thicker and sweeter and has a more intense flavor. When buying soy sauce, always look at the ingredients. There should be only four: soybeans, wheat, water, and salt. Some soy sauces are chemically brewed with hydrogenated soy protein and contain caramel coloring and flavoring. Kikkoman is a delicious, naturally brewed soy sauce that is probably available at your local grocery store.

Greek Salad

Because the Olive Salad used to make the Mediterranean Wrap (see chapter 3) is so delicious, it seemed like a good idea to use it in the Greek Salad as well. Adding a piece of grilled fish makes this a full meal, known as Ouita's Favorite on the Wallace Station menu.

12 cups mixed lettuce (romaine and baby greens)

1 cup Mary's Italian Vinaigrette (recipe follows)

4 ounces sliced cucumbers (English hothouse or small pickling)

1 cup Feta cheese, crumbled

1 cup grape tomato halves

1 cup roasted red pepper strips

1 cup Olive Salad (see index)

Thinly sliced red onion, to taste

1 cup Country Croutons (recipe follows)

For each serving: Place 2 large handfuls (about 3 cups) salad greens in a large bowl, add ¼ cup vinaigrette, and toss gently with salad tongs. Mound dressed greens on a large plate or in a shallow bowl and garnish with 1 ounce sliced cucumbers, ¼ cup Feta cheese, ¼ cup grape tomato halves, ¼ cup roasted red peppers, ¼ cup Olive Salad, several red onion rings, and ¼ cup croutons. Repeat with remaining ingredients.

Serves 4.

Country Croutons

These croutons have a neutral flavor profile, but they can be tailored to enhance a salad by adding dried herbs, garlic powder, or even Parmesan cheese toward the end of the baking time. Using day-old or stale bread makes cutting easier and gives new life to those last few slices. For salads, a ½-inch cube works best.

4 cups cubed firm-textured bread (Italian or sourdough)

3–4 tablespoons olive oil

Salt and pepper to taste

Preheat oven to 350 degrees F.

Toss bread cubes with olive oil, then season with salt and pepper. Pour onto a baking sheet in a single layer. Bake 10 minutes and stir. Return to the oven for another 5 minutes or until crisp and light golden brown.

Mary's Italian Vinaigrette

Mary Parlanti is a tiny redheaded Irish lady who really knows how to cook Italian food. Her husband, Vic, is Italian, and she learned his family's recipes from her mother-in-law. Retired now, Mary led the kitchen of Amato's Italian restaurant in the early 1990s and had her own successful business, the Kitchen at Chevy Chase. I went to school with Mary's children, and we became good friends when Chris and I bought Holly Hill Inn. Twice, Mary has been the guest chef there, on one occasion making almost 500 tamales from her mother's recipe for a large restaurant dine-around event. Mary has shared her recipes for Italian cream cake, rum custard torte, sausages, and secret sauces, including this Italian vinaigrette, which knocked me out with its punch and flavor. Mary gave me permission to use the vinaigrette on the Wallace Station menu, and it has been a mainstay ever since.

½ cup red wine vinegar

¼ cup finely chopped red onion

1–2 garlic cloves, minced

1½ teaspoons dried oregano

1 teaspoon freshly ground black pepper

1½ teaspoons kosher salt

½ teaspoon sugar

2 tablespoons Dijon mustard

1 cup canola oil

Combine all ingredients except oil in a food processor. Pulse to chop and mix well. With the processor running, slowly drizzle in oil so that it emulsifies. Taste for seasoning and chill for at least 30 minutes before serving to allow flavors to blend.

Makes about 1¾ cups.

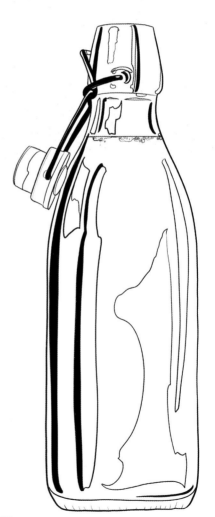

7

Brownies, Bars, and Cookies

The first three words out of my mouth as a toddler were candy, cookie, and gum. According to my parents, I would wander through the married students' housing complex where we lived, going door to door asking for treats. It was the beginning of my lifelong love affair with cookies.

My grandmother, Ouita Z. Peyton, made cookies every week and always had a freezer full of her favorites, tucked away in resealable plastic bags. Every day after lunch with my grandma, I would get two cookies for dessert, and I still believe this is the perfect finish to a sandwich lunch. A big piece of cake or a plated dessert takes too much commitment. And a cookie or a brownie can easily be tucked into a napkin for nibbling later, no fork required.

These sweets are easy to make, and they always bring a smile, no matter one's age. It is a joy to watch folks peer into the old bakery cases we use at our restaurants, looking for a treat to share.

BROWNIES
AND BARS

THE

MIDWAY

-BAKERY-

Glazed Lemon Bars

My husband, Chris, has always loved lemon bars, and this recipe is inspired by his childhood favorite: Lucy's Lemon Squares in the *Peanuts Cookbook* he bought at the Scholastic Book Fair in elementary school. Freda Raglin of Midway introduced me to lemon bars years ago at Dupree Catering. She is an amazing baker, and her lemon bars were legendary. They were so sweet and so sour that your eyes popped out a little with the first bite. She has given Wallace Station's recipe the Freda stamp of approval but finds it difficult to finish one because they are so big! The bakers at Wallace Station tinkered with Lucy's and Freda's recipes until they found one that did them both justice. The key is good lemon juice, and lots of it.

CRUST

1 cup all-purpose flour

⅓ cup powdered sugar

¼ teaspoon iodized salt

½ cup (1 stick) cold unsalted butter, cut into small pieces

1 teaspoon grated lemon zest (from 1 large lemon)

FILLING

4 large eggs

1¼ cups sugar

⅓ cup all-purpose flour

1 teaspoon baking powder

⅔ cup fresh lemon juice (from 3–4 lemons)

2 teaspoons grated lemon zest (from 2 large lemons)

GLAZE

1 cup powdered sugar

1½ tablespoons fresh lemon juice

Preheat oven to 350 degrees F. Prepare a 9-by-9-inch baking pan with nonstick spray.

For the shortbread crust: Add flour, sugar, and salt to a food processor and pulse briefly to combine. Distribute butter pieces and lemon zest over the mixture and pulse to break up the butter, about 10 short pulses. Process until large clumps of dough form. Press dough into the prepared baking pan, using flour-coated fingers or the bottom of a glass to get an even, uniform layer. Prick dough all over with a fork. Bake 20–25 minutes, until fully set and just starting to brown at the edges. Cool slightly while preparing the filling.

For the filling: In a medium bowl, whisk all filling ingredients together and pour evenly over baked and cooled crust. Bake at 350 degrees F for 25–30 minutes, or until the filling is set and the top is light brown in places. Cool to room temperature.

For the glaze and finish: Whisk powdered sugar and lemon juice together in a small bowl, then spread evenly over cooled bars. Refrigerate at least 2 hours.

Cut into 16 small squares or 6 large rectangles for Midway Bakery–size bars.

Danger Brownies

Stella Parks made the first Danger Brownie, which included a bourbon truffle on top and contained almost a pound of chocolate. Over the years, we have tinkered with her recipe to make it more economical, but the first version was legendary. Customers have said that it can take them two days to finish a Danger Brownie—eating one little square at a time.

BROWNIE

6 ounces bittersweet chocolate chunks

1 cup (2 sticks) plus 2 tablespoons unsalted butter

1½ cups sugar

4 large eggs

1½ teaspoons pure vanilla extract

½ cup unsweetened cocoa powder

1 cup all-purpose flour

1 cup chopped toasted English walnuts (see note below)

FROSTING

8 ounces semisweet chocolate chips

½ cup heavy whipping cream

¾–1 cup sifted powdered sugar

Preheat oven to 350 degrees F. Prepare a 13-by-9-inch pan with nonstick spray.

Melt bittersweet chocolate and butter in a small saucepan over low heat and stir until smooth. Remove from heat and let cool.

Pour cooled chocolate mixture into a large bowl. By hand, stir in sugar, eggs, and vanilla.

Blend well. Sift cocoa and flour together and add slowly to the chocolate mixture, stirring until incorporated. Fold in toasted walnuts.

Pour batter into the prepared pan and level with a spatula. Bake 30–35 minutes. Do not overbake—these brownies are fudgy and dense. Brownies should begin to pull away from the sides of the pan at the top and should be firm to the touch but not solid. Remove from the oven and cool to room temperature.

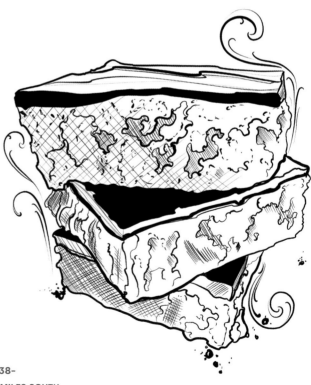

While brownies are cooling, prepare the frosting. Heat chocolate chips and whipping cream together in a small saucepan and whisk until smooth. Beat in powdered sugar until the mixture is spreadable. Pour over cooled brownies and smooth with a spatula. Cool completely and cut into 24 squares.

Note: To toast nuts, spread them in a single layer on a baking sheet. Bake at 350 degrees F for 8–12 minutes, shaking halfway through to stir. The nuts should be light brown and sweetly aromatic. Cool before adding to the recipe.

I met Stella Parks when she was a high school student with a passion for cooking and especially baking. Her mom and dad brought her to Holly Hill Inn for dinner on special occasions. Stella's graduation from the Culinary Institute of America (Chris's and my alma mater) coincided with the opening of Wallace Station in July 2003, and she became our first pastry chef. At the time, she was obsessed with chocolate—hence the Danger Brownie. Stella went on to become a very successful pastry chef and created a blog called *BraveTart*. Her best-selling cookbook, *BraveTart: Iconic American Desserts*, won the James Beard Foundation's Book Award for Baking and Desserts in 2018. I have always been proud that some of her early work was at Wallace Station.

Lolos

Lora Ginter made these bars at Wallace Station one day, basing her recipe on the old Hello Dolly seven-layer bar. Lora's extra-deep bars were such a hit that we named them for her—Lolo. We bought special deep baking pans just to make Lolos, and the "lolo pan" has become part of our bakery vernacular.

½ cup (1 stick) unsalted butter

¼ cup sugar

2 cups graham cracker crumbs

1 (12-ounce) bag white chocolate chips

1 (12-ounce) bag semisweet chocolate chips

2 cups chopped toasted nuts (pecans or walnuts)

2 cups sweetened shredded coconut

2 (14-ounce) cans sweetened condensed milk

Preheat oven to 350 degrees F. Prepare a 13-by-9-inch baking pan with nonstick spray.

Melt butter and mix with sugar and graham cracker crumbs. Press mixture into the prepared pan.

Layer remaining ingredients in the order listed.

Bake 30–35 minutes, until sides are bubbly and brown.

Cut into 24 bars when still slightly warm and remove from the pan.

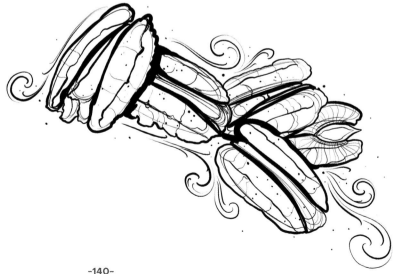

Cheesecake Brownies

With this recipe, we're expressing Chris's New York heritage by swirling cheesecake batter with our famous brownie batter.

BROWNIE

6 ounces bittersweet chocolate chunks

1 cup (2 sticks) plus 2 tablespoons unsalted butter

1½ cups sugar

4 large eggs

1½ teaspoons pure vanilla extract

½ cup unsweetened cocoa powder

1 cup all-purpose flour

CHEESECAKE

6 ounces cream cheese, at room temperature

4 tablespoons (½ stick) unsalted butter, at room temperature

½ cup sugar

1 large egg

1 teaspoon pure vanilla extract

2 tablespoons all-purpose flour

Preheat oven to 350 degrees F. Prepare a 13-by-9-inch pan with nonstick spray.

For the brownie: In a small saucepan, melt chocolate and butter over low heat and stir until smooth. Remove from heat and let cool.

Pour cooled chocolate mixture into a large bowl. By hand, stir in sugar, eggs, and vanilla. Blend well. Sift cocoa and flour together and add slowly to the chocolate mixture, stirring until incorporated.

Pour batter into the prepared pan, reserving 1 cup for the top. Level with a spatula. Set aside.

For the cheesecake: In a small mixing bowl, beat cream cheese and butter until smooth. Add remaining ingredients and mix well.

Distribute cheesecake batter evenly over brownie batter, then spoon reserved brownie batter on top. Swirl with a knife to marble the batters.

Bake 30–35 minutes. Do not overbake—these brownies are fudgy and dense. Brownies should begin to pull away from the sides of the pan at the top and should be firm to the touch but not solid. Remove from the oven and cool to room temperature.

Cut into 24 squares.

Mallory's Banana Blondies

Mallory Pfiester Martinez loves all things banana. As manager of the Midway Bakery, she had ample opportunity to use bananas in cupcakes, scones, cookies, and layer cakes. Sara Gibbs brought her a special treat whenever her local grocery store had a "Banana Wednesday" promotion—10 pounds for $1. These blondies, like most baked goods using bananas, are best when made with bananas that are turning black and very fragrant. Ripe bananas can be peeled and frozen in plastic bags for later use.

BARS

½ cup (1 stick) unsalted butter, melted

1 cup light brown sugar, lightly packed

1 large egg

1½ teaspoons pure vanilla extract

½ cup mashed very ripe banana (1–2 bananas, depending on size)

¼ teaspoon iodized salt

1 cup all-purpose flour

BROWN BUTTER GLAZE

4 tablespoons (½ stick) unsalted butter

¾ teaspoon pure vanilla extract

¼ teaspoon ground cinnamon

1⅔ cups powdered sugar

1½ tablespoons whole milk

Preheat oven to 350 degrees F. Line an 8-by-8-inch pan with parchment or foil, then spray with nonstick spray.

For the bars: Combine the first 5 ingredients in a large bowl, then fold in salt and flour until smooth. Spread in the prepared pan. Bake for 25–30 minutes, until the center is set. Do not overbake, or the bars will be tough. Remove from the oven and cool to room temperature.

For the glaze: Melt butter in a saucepan over medium heat and continue to cook, swirling the butter, until it turns golden brown and smells nutty. Pour into a bowl and add vanilla and cinnamon. Beat in powdered sugar and milk. If the glaze is too thin, add powdered sugar; if too thick, add milk. Spread evenly over cooled bars.

Cut into 16 small or 9 large bars.

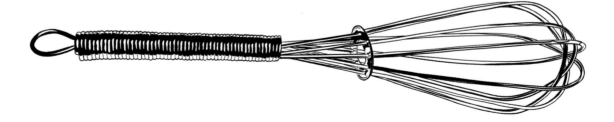

Cranberry Streusel Bars

USA Today featured the Midway Bakery and the Cranberry Streusel Bar in 2014.

SHORTBREAD

1½ cups all-purpose flour

½ cup sugar

¼ teaspoon iodized salt

½ cup (1 stick) plus 2 tablespoons cold unsalted butter, cut into small pieces

¾ teaspoon grated orange zest (from 1 medium orange)

FILLING

8 ounces fresh or frozen cranberries

¾ cup sugar

¼ cup cold water or orange juice

1 teaspoon packed grated orange zest (from 1 medium orange)

STREUSEL

⅓ cup all-purpose flour

⅓ cup old-fashioned rolled oats

⅓ cup light brown sugar, lightly packed

⅓ cup sugar

¼ teaspoon iodized salt

4 tablespoons (½ stick) cold unsalted butter, cut into small pieces

½ cup slivered almonds (about 2 ounces)

Preheat oven to 350 degrees F and position a rack in the middle. Cut an 8-by-16-inch piece of parchment paper and line an 8-by-8-inch baking pan so that the two long ends of the parchment hang over the edges of the pan. Smooth the parchment, pressing it into the corners.

For the shortbread: Add flour, sugar, and salt to a food processor and pulse briefly to combine. Distribute butter pieces and orange zest over the mixture and pulse to break up the butter, about 10 short pulses. Process until large clumps of dough form.

Press dough into the prepared baking pan, using the bottom of a flour-coated cup or glass to get an even, uniform layer. Prick dough all over with a fork. Bake about 25 minutes, until fully set and just starting to brown at the edges. While the shortbread is baking, make the filling and streusel.

For the filling: Place cranberries, sugar, and water or juice in a medium saucepan over medium-high heat and bring to a boil, stirring occasionally. Reduce heat to medium-low and simmer until cranberries have popped and are beginning to break down and the liquid has started to thicken into a syrup, about 8 minutes. Remove pan from heat and stir in orange zest. Cool slightly, about 10 minutes.

For the streusel: Whisk flour, oats, sugars, and salt in a medium bowl until combined. Add butter pieces and, using your fingers, work them into the dry mixture until large clumps form and all the flour and oats are mixed into the butter, about 5 minutes. Add almonds and, using your fingers, mix in thoroughly. Break the streusel into pieces about the size of a nickel. Refrigerate until ready to use.

To assemble the bar: When shortbread is done, remove pan from the oven and place on a wire rack. Reduce oven temperature to 325 degrees F. Pour cooled filling over hot shortbread and spread evenly. Sprinkle streusel evenly over the top and gently press into filling. Bake until filling is bubbling and streusel is golden brown, 25–30 minutes. Cool on a wire rack for at least 30 minutes so filling can set.

To remove from the pan, run a paring knife along the two exposed edges of the pan, grip the parchment handles, and pull the bars out of the pan. Transfer to a cutting board and cool completely, about 30 minutes. Remove and discard the parchment.

Cut into 16 small (2-by-2-inch) squares or 6 large (2-by-4-inch) rectangles for Midway Bakery–size bars.

Chocolate Bourbon Pecan Pie Bars

In January 2017, I served as honorary chef for the Bluegrass Ball hosted by the Kentucky Society of Washington, DC, as part of the presidential inaugural festivities. The menu was inspired by Kentucky's rich culinary history and featured local products and produce. The Midway Bakery staff baked enough of these bars (based on our popular Chocolate Bourbon Pecan Pie; see chapter 8) to serve 800 people, packed them snugly in pizza boxes, and stacked them carefully in the truck that transported them to Washington. They are a great addition to a Derby party dessert table or any sweets table where a Kentucky-style dessert can shine.

CRUST

1¾ cups all-purpose flour

¾ cup (1½ sticks) unsalted butter, at room temperature

⅓ cup sugar

¼ teaspoon iodized salt

FILLING

4 ounces bittersweet chocolate chunks or chips

4 tablespoons (½ stick) unsalted butter

4 large eggs

1 cup light brown sugar, lightly packed

6 tablespoons all-purpose flour

1 teaspoon iodized salt

1½ cups light corn syrup

1 teaspoon pure vanilla extract

2 tablespoons Kentucky bourbon

2 cups pecan pieces

Preheat oven to 350 degrees F. Prepare a 13-by-9-inch baking pan with nonstick spray.

For the crust: Combine all ingredients in the bowl of an electric mixer. Beat on medium speed until the mixture resembles coarse crumbs. Press evenly into the bottom of the prepared pan. Bake 15 minutes, or until edges are lightly browned. Remove from the oven and set aside.

For the filling: While the crust is baking, place chocolate chunks and butter in a heatproof bowl and melt in a microwave on medium power. Stir well until butter and chocolate are melted and well combined. Set aside.

Place eggs in a large bowl and beat well. Add brown sugar, flour, salt, corn syrup, vanilla, and bourbon and whisk thoroughly until well combined. Add melted chocolate mixture and pecans and whisk thoroughly. Pour evenly over the warm, partially baked crust. Bake 30–35 minutes, or until filling is set. Cool completely and refrigerate.

Cut into 48 bars.

COOKIES

Woodford Chocolate Oatmeal Cookies

Sara Gibbs created this cookie to serve at the Woodford Reserve Distillery Visitor's Center. The flavors represent all five segments of the bourbon flavor wheel, so the cookie is a perfect complement to a shot of good Kentucky bourbon, a cup of coffee, or a glass of cold milk. We include the Woodford cookie in my Bourbon Lover's Cookie Box from the Midway Bakery (see page 166).

2 cups all-purpose flour

⅓ cup cocoa powder

1 teaspoon baking soda

1 teaspoon iodized salt

¾ teaspoon ground cinnamon

½ teaspoon ground nutmeg

1 cup (2 sticks) unsalted butter, at room temperature

1 cup sugar

1 cup dark brown sugar, lightly packed

2 large eggs

2 teaspoons pure vanilla extract

1 cup old-fashioned rolled oats

1 cup coarsely chopped bittersweet chocolate or bittersweet baking chips

1 cup toasted chopped pecans

1 cup dried cranberries

Preheat oven to 350 degrees F. Line baking sheets with parchment.

Whisk together flour, cocoa, baking soda, salt, cinnamon, and nutmeg in a large bowl. Set aside.

In the bowl of an electric mixer, beat butter and sugars together just until well blended.

Add eggs and vanilla and beat until thoroughly mixed. Add oats and chocolate and mix again. Add flour mixture, mixing well. Stir in nuts and dried cranberries.

Drop 1½-ounce scoops (2 tablespoons) of dough onto parchment-lined baking sheets, 1½ inches apart. Chill 15 minutes. Bake until toasted on the edges but still moist in the center, about 15 minutes. Transfer to racks to cool. The cookies will flatten out and will be moist and chewy on the inside and crisp on the outside.

Makes about 46 (3-inch) cookies.

Flavor wheels are used to describe the flavors found in complex foods and beverages. The one for Woodford Reserve Distiller's Select Bourbon has five equal parts, each of which is represented by an ingredient in the recipe for Woodford Chocolate Oatmeal Cookies. Toasted nuts provide the earthy wood notes, rolled oats contribute an underlying malty biscuit note, vanilla and chocolate offer sweet aromatics, ground cinnamon and cocoa provide the depth and complexity of spice, and cranberries supply a fruit and floral finish.

JUMBO COOKIES

In the beginning, Wallace Station was essentially a bakery. We hoped it would support Holly Hill Inn's dessert production as well as sell its own line of handmade baked goods. Little did we know how it would explode. From 2003 to 2011, when we opened the Midway Bakery, Wallace Station produced breads, brownies, muffins, and cookies in its small kitchen while selling hundreds of griddled sandwiches each week. Jumbo cookies were on the menu from day one. Many of the recipes were created in the early days by Stella Parks, Clay McClure, and Jared Richardson. The recipes here have been formulated for traditional-size cookies baked in home ovens.

Walnut Chocolate Chip Cookies

Toasting the walnuts before adding them to the batter enhances their flavor. Substitute other varieties of nuts if you like, or omit the nuts altogether.

1 cup (2 sticks) unsalted butter, at room temperature

¾ cup light brown sugar, lightly packed

½ cup sugar

2 large eggs

1 teaspoon pure vanilla extract

1 teaspoon baking soda

¾ teaspoon iodized salt

2½ cups all-purpose flour

1 (12-ounce) bag semisweet chocolate chips

1¼ cups chopped toasted walnut pieces

Preheat oven to 350 degrees F. Prepare baking sheets with nonstick spray or cover with parchment.

Cream butter and sugars. Add eggs and vanilla and beat well. Stir baking soda and salt into flour and then add to butter mixture. Mix well with an electric mixer on low speed, scraping the bowl and beaters. Stir in chocolate chips and walnut pieces.

Drop 2-ounce scoops (¼ cup) of dough onto prepared baking sheets, 3 inches apart. Flatten slightly. Each cookie will spread to about 4 inches during baking. Bake 18–20 minutes, rotating baking sheets halfway through. The tops should be light brown around the edges, and the bottoms will be golden brown.

Remove from the oven and cool for about 1 minute. Using a metal spatula, move cookies to cooling racks.

Makes about 27 (4-inch) cookies.

White Chocolate Peanut Butter Cookies

1¼ cups creamy peanut butter

1 cup (2 sticks) unsalted butter, at room temperature

1 cup sugar

1 cup light brown sugar, lightly packed

2 large eggs

1 teaspoon pure vanilla extract

1½ teaspoons baking soda

1½ teaspoons iodized salt

2¾ cups all-purpose flour

1 (12-ounce) bag white chocolate chunks or chips

Preheat oven to 375 degrees F. Line baking sheets with parchment.

Cream peanut butter, butter, and sugars until fluffy. Add eggs and vanilla and mix well with an electric mixer on medium speed. On low speed, mix in baking soda and salt, then slowly add flour until well combined. Add white chocolate chunks or chips.

Use a scoop to portion dough into 36 balls. Roll into balls about 1½ inches in diameter and place on parchment-covered baking sheets, leaving plenty of space for cookies to spread, about 8 cookies per sheet. Flatten with a fork, making a crisscross pattern.

Bake 15–17 minutes, or until cookies begin to brown. Rotate baking sheets halfway through. Do not overbake. Cookies should still be slightly soft in the center.

Makes about 36 (3-inch) cookies.

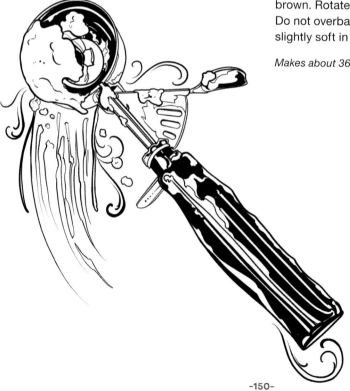

⚜ Ginger Gems

These spicy cookies, from a recipe by Lisa Laufer, differ from the norm with the addition of fresh lemon zest, which sharpens the flavor.

1½ cups (3 sticks) unsalted butter, at room temperature

1¾ cups light brown sugar, lightly packed

½ cup molasses

2 large eggs

2 tablespoons grated lemon zest (from 4 large lemons)

3 tablespoons ground ginger

1½ tablespoons ground cinnamon

1 teaspoon iodized salt

1 tablespoon plus 1 teaspoon baking soda

5 cups all-purpose flour

Preheat oven to 350 degrees F. Line baking sheets with parchment.

Cream butter and brown sugar until light and fluffy. Add molasses and blend well. Add eggs and lemon zest and mix well. Add dry ingredients and mix until well incorporated.

Use a scoop to portion dough into 36 balls (about 1½ ounces or 2 tablespoons each). Roll into balls and place on parchment-lined baking sheets, leaving plenty of space for cookies to spread, about 8 cookies per sheet. Flatten slightly with a floured hand.

Bake 12–14 minutes, rotating baking sheets halfway through. Cool on pans until cookies begin to firm up, then transfer to wire cooling racks.

Makes about 36 (3-inch) cookies.

To make about 82 smaller (2-inch) cookies, drop tablespoons of dough on prepared baking sheets and bake 11–12 minutes. These cookies freeze beautifully and pack well in boxes to give as gifts.

Oatmeal Raisin Cookies

Oatmeal raisin cookies are my favorite. They take me back to those crazy lunches Mom used to pack for us. Her oatmeal raisin cookies were dense, packed with oats and probably four other grains we knew nothing about. She was always trying to make everything we ate super healthy, even our treats.

1 cup (2 sticks) unsalted butter, at room temperature

1 cup light brown sugar, lightly packed

½ cup sugar

2 large eggs

¾ teaspoon pure vanilla extract

1 teaspoon baking soda

½ teaspoon ground cinnamon

½ teaspoon iodized salt

3 cups old-fashioned rolled oats

1½ cups raisins

1½ cups all-purpose flour

Preheat oven to 350 degrees F. Prepare baking sheets with a light coating of nonstick spray.

Cream butter and sugars in the bowl of an electric mixer on medium-high speed until light and fluffy. Add eggs, one at a time, beating well after each addition. Stir in vanilla.

In a small bowl, stir together baking soda, cinnamon, salt, and oats. Add to butter mixture and mix until well incorporated. Add raisins. Scrape the bowl and beaters and mix again. Add flour with the mixer on low speed. Blend well.

Scoop dough by heaping tablespoons (about 1 ounce) and drop on the prepared baking sheets, about 3 inches apart. Flatten slightly. Bake 14 minutes, rotating baking sheets halfway through. Cool on pans about 5 minutes before removing to cooling racks.

Makes about 42 cookies.

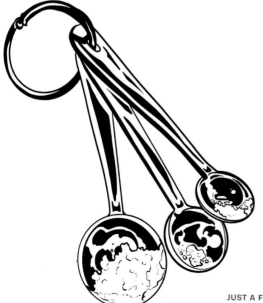

8

Pie Supper

Pie suppers became popular in the Ozark Mountains and throughout Appalachia after the Civil War. Eligible young ladies made pies that would be auctioned to raise money to support churches or other community endeavors. Often, each young lady would share her pie with the highest bidder, resulting in many pie supper romances. These community celebrations, which often included music and square dancing, provided a chance for those living on surrounding small farms to socialize.

continued

Midway Christian Church (Disciples of Christ) has hosted a few pie suppers over the years, and my friends Jim and Jan Nance always command the top price for their secret-recipe chocolate bourbon hickory nut pie. Jim gathers and shells the nuts himself. I have been outbid on that pie more than once!

One of my favorite pie-related experiences involved teaching our Kids in the Kitchen cooking class at church how to make pie. The students, who ranged in age from five to twelve years old, made their own crusts and fillings and then baked their pie creations. Parents were worried about the mess, and the bottom of the oven saw quite a bit of dripping and smoking, but it's safe to say that we all ate the best pies of our parenting lives that afternoon. When I was a little girl, I remember standing at the elbow of my grandmother Ouita Peyton and watching as she stretched her pie rolling cloth and readied her rolling pin. She would give me extra bits of dough and let me roll them out to make a tiny crust in a baby pie pan. Then we'd fill it with sugar and butter—and she'd call me her little sugar pie. My mom used that same cloth for her pie doughs, and I can see her in my mind's eye when my daughter, Willa, makes a little sugar pie just like I did. Pie has always been one of my favorite dishes and desserts.

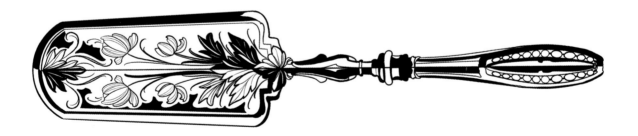

When we were preparing for the opening of the Midway School Bakery, Carrie Warmbier, pastry chef at Holly Hill Inn, and I tested several pie recipes. We put six pies on the dessert menu and gave folks an option: have one piece of pie for dessert or choose the pie supper and get a piece of all six. We were shocked by the number of folks who ordered the pie supper. We still love to offer pie supper at Holly Hill Inn and at special events we cater.

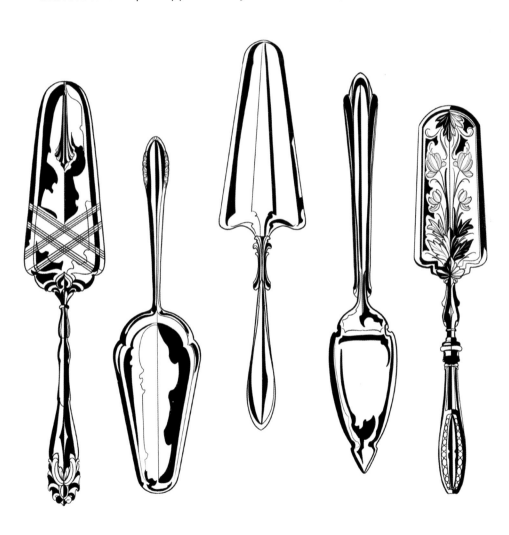

Midway Bakery All-Butter Pie Crust

This pie crust has been used at the Midway Bakery since it opened in 2011. Instead of ice water, the bakers use cold milk for added fat and a little vinegar for tenderness. Although the staff at the bakery gently works the butter in by hand when making huge batches, this one-crust recipe can be mixed in a food processor.

1 cup all-purpose flour

¼ teaspoon iodized salt

½ cup (1 stick) cold unsalted butter, cut into small pieces

½ teaspoon cider vinegar

2½–4 tablespoons cold whole milk

Add flour and salt to a food processor and pulse several times to combine. Add butter and pulse until it is broken into very small pieces and the mixture resembles coarse meal. Add vinegar and then slowly pour in milk, pulsing until the dough comes together. Remove from the processor and knead on a floured surface several times. Pat into a disk, wrap in plastic wrap, and refrigerate at least 30 minutes before using.

Makes 1 (9-inch) pie crust.

For 2 crusts, follow the directions above using 2 cups flour, ½ teaspoon salt, 1 cup (2 sticks) unsalted butter, 1 teaspoon cider vinegar, and ⅓–½ cup milk.

To blind-bake a pie crust, roll out the dough, line a pie pan with it, flute the edges, and prick the bottom all over with a fork. Freeze the crust in the pan for at least 30 minutes. While the crust is freezing, preheat the oven to 375 degrees F.

Remove the crust from the freezer and line it with parchment paper, allowing about 2 inches to hang over the sides to serve as handles for lifting. Make sure to fit the parchment snugly into the angle where the bottom meets the sides. Fill the pan to the top with uncooked dry beans or rice or ceramic pie weights. Bake 25 minutes. Using the parchment handles, remove the weights from the pie, reduce the temperature to 325 degrees F, and continue baking 15 minutes, until the crust has dried out and is light golden brown. Allow it to cool to room temperature before continuing with the recipe. The rice or beans can be reused as pie weights many times.

Mabel's Lemon Cake Pie

When we started discussing ideas for desserts at Honeywood, Sara Gibbs went to work. She searched her vast cookbook collection, but nothing seemed quite right. Next, she turned to the internet and spent hours reviewing pies with bourbon and without, pies with streusel toppings, pies with lattice crust, shortbread crust, and graham cracker crust. Nothing spoke to her. Eventually, she turned to a family cookbook that her mother, Mabel Lyons Thompson, had compiled in the 1970s on a manual typewriter. "It has become my culinary bible and eventually grew to two volumes," Sara said. "In retrospect, that is where I should have started. Finally, I found the recipe that seemed to have endless possibilities: Lemon Cake Pie."

This pie was a favorite of Sara's father. Her family ate it with strawberries in the spring and blueberries in the summer, but always with whipped cream. It is light yet profoundly satisfying, and it seems to embody a bit of culinary magic. The filling somehow separates into layers while baking, resulting in a creamy, tangy custard on the bottom and a light chiffon cake layer on top.

1 recipe Midway Bakery All-Butter Pie Crust, blind baked (see page 156)

1 cup sugar

2 tablespoons all-purpose flour

1 tablespoon unsalted butter, melted

¼ teaspoon iodized salt

Grated zest of 1 lemon (about ½ teaspoon)

⅓ cup fresh lemon juice

2 large egg whites

3 large egg yolks

1 cup whole milk

Preheat oven to 400 degrees F. Move oven rack to the lowest position.

In a medium bowl, stir together sugar, flour, butter, salt, lemon zest, and lemon juice. Set aside.

In another medium bowl, beat egg whites with an electric mixer until they hold distinct but moist peaks. Set aside.

In a small bowl, beat egg yolks and milk until well blended, then stir into the lemon mixture. Gently fold egg whites into the lemon mixture. Don't overmix. Pour filling into cooled crust.

Bake 10 minutes, then reduce temperature to 325 degrees F and bake until the top is lightly browned and the center jiggles only slightly when gently shaken, about 30 minutes. If the crust begins to brown too much, drape it with foil and continue baking. Cool to room temperature, then refrigerate before serving.

Makes 1 (9-inch) pie.

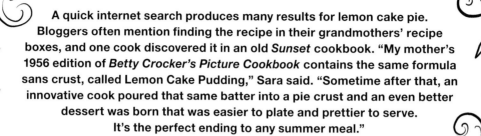
Spiced Pecan Pie

After visiting the Texas Hill Country along the Blanco River, Sara Gibbs developed a love for Texas pecans, where formerly only Georgia pecans would do. This recipe is based on one published in *Texas Monthly* magazine and is different from the too-sweet versions found on most tables. The spices and dark corn syrup give the pie a deeper and more complex flavor, especially when topped with a dollop of homemade whipped cream.

1 recipe Midway Bakery All-Butter Pie Crust (see page 156)

½ cup sugar

1 cup dark corn syrup

4 tablespoons (½ stick) unsalted butter, cut into small pieces

3 large eggs, lightly beaten

1½ cups coarsely chopped pecans

1 teaspoon pure vanilla extract

½ teaspoon ground cloves

½ teaspoon ground allspice

1 teaspoon ground cinnamon

¼ teaspoon iodized salt

24–36 pecan halves

Preheat oven to 375 degrees F.

Roll out the pie crust, fit it into a 9-inch pie pan, and flute the edges. Chill until ready to fill.

Bring sugar and corn syrup to a boil, remove from heat, and stir in butter. Cool to room temperature. Stir in eggs, chopped pecans, vanilla, cloves, allspice, cinnamon, and salt. Mix well and pour into prepared pie crust. Place pecan halves on top of the filling, lining the edge of the pie. Bake 40–45 minutes, covering with foil during the last 15 minutes if necessary. Cool completely before serving.

Makes 1 (9-inch) pie.

Apple Cranberry Bourbon Crunch Pie

This unique apple pie is laced with fresh cranberries, giving the filling a soft pink color as they cook down during baking. Mixing two or three varieties of apples allows the baker to balance tart with sweet, soft with firm. The splash of bourbon and the crunchy streusel topping make this pie a good choice for any holiday table.

CRUST

1 recipe Midway Bakery All-Butter Pie Crust (see page 156)

FILLING

2 pounds Granny Smith, Fuji, McIntosh, or Gala apples (use at least 2 varieties), peeled, cored, and thinly sliced (about 6 cups)

1 cup fresh or frozen cranberries

2 tablespoons bourbon

1 tablespoon fresh lemon juice

7 tablespoons all-purpose flour

½ teaspoon ground cinnamon

¼ teaspoon ground nutmeg

¼ teaspoon iodized salt

¾ cup sugar

STREUSEL

¾ cup all-purpose flour

½ cup light brown sugar, lightly packed

2 teaspoons ground cinnamon

Pinch iodized salt

6 tablespoons (¾ stick) cold unsalted butter, cut into small pieces

½ cup pecan pieces

Preheat oven to 400 degrees F. Place rack in the lower third of the oven.

Roll out the pie crust, fit it into a 9-inch pie pan, and flute the edges. Chill until ready to fill.

For the filling: In a large bowl, toss apple slices and cranberries with bourbon and lemon juice. Set aside. In a small bowl, mix together flour, cinnamon, nutmeg, salt, and sugar and add to the apples, tossing until well coated. Mound the filling in the prepared pie shell. Place on a parchment-lined baking sheet and cover loosely with foil. Bake 30 minutes.

For the streusel: While the pie is baking, place flour, brown sugar, cinnamon, and salt in a medium bowl and mix well. Using your hands, work butter into the flour mixture, squeezing it between your fingers until crumbly. Add pecan pieces and mix well.

After baking 30 minutes, remove pie from the oven, remove foil, and reduce heat to 375 degrees F. Sprinkle streusel evenly over the top and return pie to the oven for 45 minutes–1 hour, until apples can be easily pierced with a sharp knife but still have texture. If the edges brown too quickly, cover with foil and continue baking. Cool to lukewarm before serving.

Makes 1 (9-inch) pie.

Sour Cream Apple Pie

Lora Ginter first baked this recipe for Sour Cream Apple Pie at Wallace Station. The sweet, crunchy topping is perfectly balanced by the tart, creamy filling.

CRUST

1 recipe Midway Bakery All-Butter Pie Crust (see page 156)

FILLING

5 cups sliced and peeled Gala or Granny Smith apples (about 3 large)

1 cup sour cream

¾ cup sugar

½ teaspoon iodized salt

2 tablespoons all-purpose flour

1 large egg, beaten

STREUSEL

¾ cup all-purpose flour

⅓ cup light brown sugar, lightly packed

½ teaspoon ground cinnamon

¼ teaspoon iodized salt

6 tablespoons (¾ stick) frozen unsalted butter

Preheat oven to 425 degrees F.

Roll out the pie crust, fit it into a 9-inch pie pan, and flute the edges. Chill until ready to fill.

For the filling: Mix all filling ingredients and add to the unbaked pie shell. Place on a parchment-lined baking sheet to catch any drips. Bake at 425 degrees F for 15 minutes. Reduce heat to 350 degrees F and bake another 30 minutes.

For the streusel: While the pie is baking, mix dry ingredients in a small bowl, then grate frozen butter into the flour mixture and toss together by hand. Pull the pie from the oven and mound the streusel mixture on top. Return to the oven and bake an additional 30–35 minutes, until filling is bubbling and slightly spilling over the crust.

This pie is best served slightly warm or at room temperature. Refrigerate any leftovers.

Makes 1 (9-inch) pie.

Reed Valley Orchard, halfway between Cynthiana and Paris, Kentucky, has more than fifty varieties of apple trees and also grows blueberries, blackberries, black raspberries, peaches, and pumpkins. The first June apple is the Lodi, and each year we look forward to making applesauce with these pale green, tart apples. You can cook them skin and all! For pie, of course, the traditional Granny Smith always works, but I also love Jonagold, Red Spy, and Cortland apples. Rome and York apples are great for pies, too. Hiking among the apple trees at Reed Valley and along the old stagecoach trails haunted by Jesse and Frank James is a wonderful way to spend an afternoon, topped off by one of Trudie Reed's baked apple hand pies.

Peanut Butter Mousse Pie

This creamy, no-bake pie has become one of the most popular desserts at the Midway Bakery and is a favorite with diners at the Fasig-Tipton horse sales.

CRUST

1⅓ cups chocolate sandwich cookie crumbs (12 cookies)

3 tablespoons unsalted butter

Pinch iodized salt

½ teaspoon espresso powder

GANACHE

¼ cup heavy cream

½ teaspoon pure vanilla extract

½ cup semisweet chocolate chips

FILLING

1 cup cold heavy whipping cream

1 (8-ounce) package cream cheese, at room temperature

1 cup creamy peanut butter

1 cup powdered sugar

For the crust: To make crumbs, pulse 12 chocolate sandwich cookies in a food processor until the consistency resembles coarse sand. Melt butter and combine with salt, espresso powder, and cookie crumbs. Pour into a 9-inch deep-dish pie pan and press gently into the bottom and about three-quarters of the way up the sides. Set aside.

For the ganache: Place cream, vanilla, and chocolate chips in a microwavable glass bowl and heat 1 minute on 50 percent power. Stir until smooth. Spread most of the ganache over the bottom of the pie crust, reserving 2–3 tablespoons to use as garnish.

For the filling: In the bowl of an electric mixer, whip cream until stiff, scrape into another bowl, and set aside. In the mixer bowl, beat cream cheese until smooth, then beat together with peanut butter. Slowly add powdered sugar and mix until smooth and fluffy. Using a rubber spatula, fold whipped cream into the peanut butter mixture, then mound it in the prepared pie shell. Smooth the top and drizzle or pipe the remaining ganache on top (use a small plastic bag with a snipped corner or a piping bag with a small, round tip). Chill at least 4 hours before serving.

Makes 1 (9-inch) pie.

Chocolate Bourbon Pecan Pie

Western Kentucky is blessed to have a variety of native pecan trees that grow along the Mississippi River. Sweet, tender, and full of natural oils, these wild seedling pecans are smaller than the paper shell varieties but full of flavor. This pie is one of our best sellers, combining native pecans, chocolate from Ruth Hunt in Mount Sterling, Kentucky, and good bourbon. It is not a traditional recipe but rather a chocolate chess, super rich and fudgy. Bourbon Whipped Cream makes an over-the-top garnish.

---

1 recipe Midway Bakery All-Butter Pie Crust (see page 156)

4 tablespoons (½ stick) unsalted butter

½ cup bittersweet chocolate pieces

4 large eggs

1 cup light brown sugar, lightly packed

½ cup corn syrup

1 teaspoon pure vanilla extract

3 tablespoons Kentucky bourbon

½ teaspoon iodized salt

1½ cups pecan pieces

Bourbon Whipped Cream (recipe follows)

Preheat oven to 350 degrees F.

Roll out the pie crust, fit it into a 9-inch pie pan, and flute the edges. Chill until ready to fill.

Melt butter and chocolate over a double boiler or in a microwave at 50 percent power until smooth. Set aside to cool.

In a large bowl, whisk eggs until light and fluffy, then add brown sugar, corn syrup, vanilla, bourbon, and salt and stir into the chocolate mixture. Place pecan pieces in the bottom of the pie crust in an even layer, then cover with chocolate filling.

Bake 50–55 minutes, until filling is set but still slightly jiggly in the center.

Serve topped with Bourbon Whipped Cream.

Makes 1 (9-inch) pie.

We order wild seedling pecans from the Kentucky Nut Corporation in Hickman, Kentucky, and have them shipped to the bakery in thirty-pound cases. The Kentucky Nut Corporation has been in business since 1940 and offers a variety of nut products online (see page 167).

Bourbon Whipped Cream

¼ cup Kentucky bourbon

¼ cup sugar

2 cups cold heavy whipping cream

Combine bourbon and sugar in a small saucepan and simmer over medium-low heat until sugar is dissolved. Remove from heat and cool completely. Combine with very cold heavy cream in a chilled bowl. Beat with a mixer or whisk to soft peaks.

Buttermilk Chess Pie

Longtime Midway resident Tempa Endicott was a good friend to Midway natives Betty Ann Voigt and Margaret Ware Parrish. All three ladies were more than generous with their time and hospitality when we moved to Midway after purchasing Holly Hill Inn. Tempa's grandson Beau Endicott worked as the restaurant's service manager and swore by his grandmother's chess pie. We tested it and agreed that Tempa's pie was the best. This is our version of her specialty.

1 recipe Midway Bakery All-Butter Pie Crust, blind baked (see page 156)

3 large eggs

½ cup (1 stick) unsalted butter, melted and cooled

1½ cups sugar

3 tablespoons all-purpose flour

¼ teaspoon iodized salt

1 cup buttermilk

1 teaspoon pure vanilla extract

1 tablespoon fresh lemon juice

1 teaspoon ground nutmeg (optional)

Preheat oven to 350 degrees F.

In a large bowl, beat eggs until light and fluffy. Add butter, sugar, flour, and salt. Then add buttermilk, vanilla, lemon juice, and nutmeg, if desired. Mix to combine. Pour into the cooled pie shell. Bake 40 minutes, or until the center is firm and set when lightly touched.

Cool on a wire rack before serving.

Makes 1 (9-inch) pie.

Blackberry Crumble Pie

Blackberries are the state fruit of Kentucky, and they grow wild in brambles all over the countryside. They are also easy to cultivate.

CRUST

1 recipe Midway Bakery All-Butter Pie Crust (see page 156)

FILLING

1¾ pounds (about 6 cups) fresh blackberries, washed and drained

2 teaspoons fresh lemon juice

⅓ cup light brown sugar, lightly packed

½ cup sugar

½ teaspoon ground cinnamon

½ teaspoon ground ginger

½ cup cornstarch

CRUMBLE

⅔ cup old-fashioned oats

½ cup light brown sugar, lightly packed

½ cup all-purpose flour

Pinch iodized salt

6 tablespoons (¾ stick) frozen unsalted butter

Preheat oven to 375 degrees F.

Roll out the pie crust, fit it into a 9-inch pie pan, and flute the edges. Chill until ready to fill.

For the filling: In a large bowl, mix blackberries and lemon juice. In a small bowl, mix brown sugar, sugar, cinnamon, ginger, and cornstarch. Pour the sugar mixture over blackberries and mix well.

Place the prepared pie crust on a parchment-lined baking sheet. Mound the berry mixture in the crust and bake 30 minutes.

For the crumble topping: While the pie is baking, pulse oats in a food processor into a large crumb. Pour into a small bowl and combine with brown sugar, flour, and salt. Grate frozen butter into the oats mixture and toss together by hand.

After the pie has baked 30 minutes, pull it from the oven and top evenly with the crumble. Reduce heat to 350 degrees F, return the pie to the oven, and continue baking another 30–35 minutes, until the berry filling bubbles through the topping and the crumble is crisp, golden brown, and cooked through.

Cool pie to room temperature, allowing the filling to set, before serving.

Makes 1 (9-inch) pie.

Kentucky's plentiful supply of blackberries ensures an abundance of delicious blackberry jam, a key ingredient of our famous Kentucky Jam Cake. Mike Wright from Versailles, Kentucky, has long cultivated a delicious loganberry, a blackberry cultivar from the Northwest. It does extremely well in Kentucky, and we buy every berry Mike can pick, using them in muffins, pies, cobblers, and compotes.

OUITA MICHEL FAMILY OF RESTAURANTS

Holly Hill Inn, Midway,
hollyhillinn.com

Wallace Station, Versailles,
(just outside Midway),
wallacestation.com

Windy Corner Market, Lexington,
windycornermarket.com

Smithtown Seafood, Lexington,
smithtownseafood.com

Honeywood, Lexington,
honeywoodrestaurant.com

Zim's Cafe and The Thirsty Fox,
Lexington, zimscafe.com

The Midway Bakery, Midway,
themidwaybakery.com

Holly Hill Events catering, Midway,
hollyhillinn.com/catering-events

Ouitamichel.com online store
(items shipped to all 50 states)
Kentucky Proud products

Ouita's Favorite Cookie Box
by the Midway Bakery

Bourbon Lover's Cookie Box
by the Midway Bakery

Smithtown Banana Pepper Mustard

Wallace Station Bourbon Mustard

Windy Corner Super Spice

SOURCES FOR KENTUCKY PRODUCTS

ALE-8-ONE
Winchester, KY
Ale8one.com
(859) 744-3484
Locally made soda

BILL BEST
heirlooms.org
Articles about heirloom varieties
and Appalachian agriculture;
heirloom seeds for purchase

BOURBON BARREL FOODS
Louisville, KY
bourbonbarrelfoods.com
(502) 333-6103
Bourbon-smoked paprika

COUNTRY ROCK SORGHUM
Woodford County, KY
Facebook.com/Countryrocksorghum/
Sorghum available at several Ouita
Michel restaurants and other local
outlets

ELMWOOD STOCK FARM
Georgetown, KY
Elmwoodstockfarm.com
Organic, pasture-raised poultry,
lamb, beef, and pork; organic fruits
and vegetables; organic free-range
eggs; canned items, dried beans,
and cornmeal; community-supported
agriculture subscriptions available

KENTUCKY NUT CORPORATION
Hickman, KY
kykernelpecans.com
(270) 236-2662
Wild seedling pecans, sorghum

**OBERHOLTZER'S
KENTUCKY SORGHUM**
Liberty, KY
amazon.com
Pure Kentucky sorghum

RUTH HUNT CANDIES
Mount Sterling, KY
ruthhuntcandy.com
(800) 927-0302
Cream candy, bourbon balls,
and other candies

STONE CROSS FARM
Taylorsville, KY
stonecrossfarm.com
(502) 477-8561
Sausage, bacon, ground beef, ribs

WEISENBERGER MILL
Midway, KY
weisenberger.com
(859) 254-5282
Fish Batter Mix, cornmeal, flour, grits

marjoram

dill

basil

oregano

thyme

ACKNOWLEDGMENTS

Thank you for reading our book. The celebration of local farming, scratch cooking, and foodways inspires our communal table and dialogue about food. Each one of our small restaurants serves as a community gathering spot and is staffed from the surrounding neighborhood. Each has a deep pocket of regular customers who influence its style and approach, and a group of dedicated staff who bring their own stories and tastes to the table. The collaboration among these elements—place, ingredient, history, and hard work in the kitchen—is the story of our food culture. Our hope is that these recipes will be made in your own kitchen and that you will enjoy many happy times around the table with generations of family and friends.

This book was years in the making, and without the hard work of Sara Gibbs and Genie Graf, it never would have gotten to the press. Their test cooks, Julie Grant and Barb Crutchfield, were invaluable in ensuring our recipes worked for home use. Thank you to Roger E. Solt for his continuous support of all our restaurants. I am grateful daily for the team of chefs, managers, and service staff at Holly Hill Inn, Wallace Station, Windy Corner Market, Midway Bakery, Smithtown Seafood, Glenn's Creek Café, Zim's Café, and Honeywood. They all have a voice in our story.

Special thanks to my husband, Chris Michel, for stewarding us through the rocky waters of small business ownership and to our daughter, Willa Michel, for enduring two parents crazy enough to get into the restaurant business.

We hope you will come visit our beloved commonwealth. Take a drive along a beautiful Bluegrass country road and stop by. You'll be kindly welcome.

⟲ INDEX

OUITA MICHEL is a six-time James Beard Foundation Award nominee, including nominations for Outstanding Restaurateur and Best Chef Southeast. Ouita and her restaurants are regularly featured in local and national media, such as the *New York Times, Southern Living, Garden & Gun,* Food Network, and the Cooking Channel. She was a guest judge on Bravo's *Top Chef* series.

Ouita and her husband, Chris, bought the Holly Hill Inn in 2000 and opened the fine dining restaurant in May 2001. Ouita's use of locally sourced foods both helps sustain Bluegrass family farms and guarantees her customers only the freshest, best-tasting fine cuisine. The devotion to local foods is evident at her other restaurants as well: Wallace Station Deli just outside Midway, Kentucky; Windy Corner Market, Smithtown Seafood, Honeywood, Zim's Café, and the Thirsty Fox in Lexington, Kentucky; and the Midway Bakery in Midway. Ouita's catering division, Holly Hill Events, shares Kentucky-sourced cuisine and hospitality with groups of all sizes. She is former chef-in-residence at Woodford Reserve Distillery outside Versailles, Kentucky.

Her restaurants have purchased $3 million of Kentucky-grown meats, dairy products, fruits, and vegetables over the last nineteen years. Her reputation and commitment to sustainability have earned speaking invitations and awards from local, regional, and national organizations.

Ouita, Chris, and their daughter, Willa, live in a two-hundred-year-old cabin adjacent to the Holly Hill Inn.

More information is available at **ouitamichel.com**.

SARA GIBBS is a former chef as well as a recipe writer and editor. After working as a West Virginia public librarian for fifteen years, Sara moved to Kentucky to attend culinary school. She worked in several Louisville restaurants, including Lynn's Paradise Café and the corporate dining room of Brown-Forman Corporation. In 2009, Sara joined Ouita Michel's restaurant family at the Woodford Reserve Distillery, and she later helped with the opening of new restaurants and with recipe development and archiving. She is coauthor of *Southern Thighways: Thigh Recipes with a Southern Accent.*

GENIE GRAF is the special projects director at the Ouita Michel Family of Restaurants. After working as a copy editor, designer, and section editor for several newspapers, Genie started a family and began a part-time role in public relations and marketing for small businesses. She transitioned to full time after her four children were grown. Genie and her husband, Mathew, live in Midway, Kentucky.

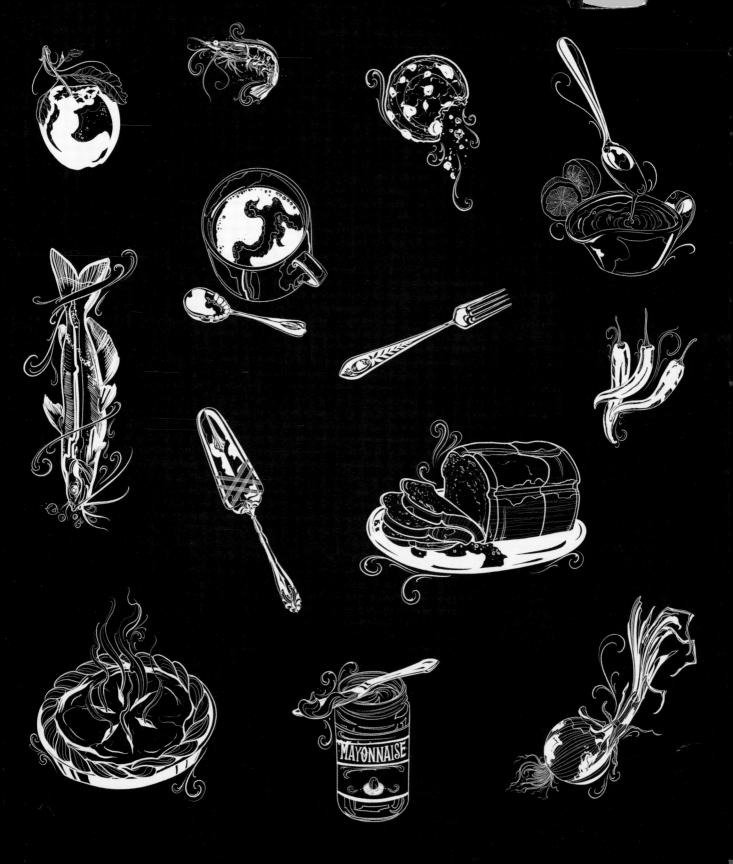